One Woman's Journey of Healing

Daddy, Please Say You're Sorry

♡Amber

CompCare® Publishers

Minneapolis, Minnesota

Library of Congress Cataloging-in-Publication Data
Amber, 1946—
     Daddy, please say you're sorry.
        p.   cm.
     ISBN 0-89638-262-1
     1. Amber, 1946 — Mental Health. 2 Incest victims —
     Mental health — Case studies.   3. Adult Child Sexual abuse
     victims — Mental health — Case studies.   I. Title.
     RC560.I53A43   1992
     616.85'83 — dc20   91-42941
                                                              CIP

Cover and interior design by Amber.

Inquiries. orders, and catalog requests should be addressed to:
CompCare Publishers
2415 Annapolis Lane
Minneapolis, Minnesota 55441
Call toll-free 1-800-328-3330
(Minnesota residents call 1-612-559-4800)

    6   5   4   3   2
    97   96   95   94   93

I want my power back...
this book is a key.

I want to empower others
...this book is a source.

♡ Amber

Dedication

To Paula ... my hope
and inspiration
for the future ...
I honor you and
love you and wish
to God I could have
protected you.

♡Amber

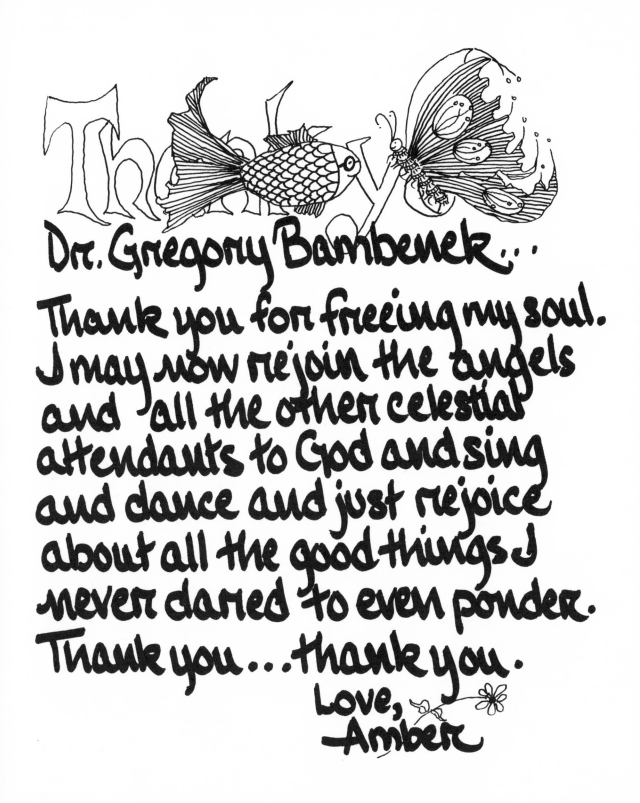

Thank You

Dr. Gregory Bambenek...

Thank you for freeing my soul.
I may now rejoin the angels
and all the other celestial
attendants to God and sing
and dance and just rejoice
about all the good things I
never dared to even ponder.
Thank you... thank you.
                    Love,
                    Amber

PREFACE

IT HAS BEEN MY PLEASURE TO
ACCOMPANY AMBER ON ONE
SEGMENT OF HER VERY LONG
JOURNEY TO HEALTH. HER JOURNEY
HAS BEEN DIFFERENT THAN THAT
OF MANY OTHERS. IT IS HER
UNIQUE WAY OF HEALING HERSELF
THAT HAS HELD SUCH APPEAL TO ME.
THIS BOOK IS A TESTIMONY TO THAT
UNIQUE FRAME OF REFERENCE
THAT IS HERS.

AS A PSYCHOTHERAPIST IT WAS MY
ROLE TO BE WITH HER AND TO LET
HER KNOW MANY TIMES THAT
SHE WAS NOT CRAZY; THAT SHE
HAD A RIGHT TO HAVE FEELINGS
AND THAT THOSE FEELINGS
WERE NOT RIGHT OR WRONG;
THAT THEY JUST WERE.

AMBER HAS GROWN FROM HER EXPERIENCES AND HAS, BY OFFERING THIS BOOK TO ALL OF US, ENRICHED US AND GIVEN US ANOTHER TOOL TO USE IN HELPING TO HEAL OTHER CHILDREN WHO HAVE BEEN VIOLATED.

THANK YOU, AMBER.

SHIRLEY LEVINE
PSYCHOTHERAPIST

i love you, Shirley...it's so nice to be cured. ~Amber

Introduction

BEING AN ARTIST CAN HAVE ITS
COMPLICATIONS. BEING AN ARTIST
CAUGHT UP IN MENTAL ILLNESS
AND THE REPERCUSSIONS OF A
DISTORTED CHILDHOOD CAN BE
EVEN MORE COMPLEX.

HAVING BEEN A VICTIM OF INCEST,
I HAVE SURVIVED INTELLECTUAL,
SPIRITUAL, PHYSICAL, AND
EMOTIONAL ABUSES. EACH HAS
TAKEN ITS TOLL.

THE PRIMARY OBJECTIVE OF THIS
BOOK HAS BEEN MY OWN
HEALING PROCESS... TO ALLOW
MYSELF TO BECOME THE

"SURVIVOR." TO NO LONGER THINK OF MYSELF AS THE "VICTIM."

AT THE TIME I BEGAN THIS BOOK, I HAD BEEN IN THERAPY THIRTEEN YEARS, AND RARELY HAD INCEST BEEN MENTIONED. THE SUBJECT WAS UNRESOLVED. I REALIZED I HAD TO TAKE THE INITIATIVE TO EXPLORE IT AND, FINALLY, TO GET ON WITH MY LIFE. THERE IS STILL MUCH TO DO.

I RECOGNIZE THAT I CANNOT SEPARATE THE FACTUAL FROM THE EMOTIONAL ASPECTS OF MY EXPERIENCES. THERE IS A BLURRING OF EMOTION AND INTELLECT IN THIS BOOK, AS THERE IS IN ME.

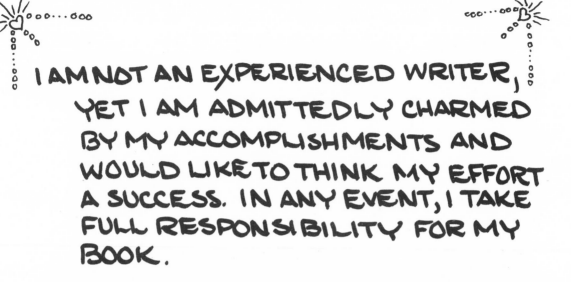

I AM NOT AN EXPERIENCED WRITER, YET I AM ADMITTEDLY CHARMED BY MY ACCOMPLISHMENTS AND WOULD LIKE TO THINK MY EFFORT A SUCCESS. IN ANY EVENT, I TAKE FULL RESPONSIBILITY FOR MY BOOK.

IF THIS BOOK CAN HELP EVEN ONE PERSON WHO HAS BEEN ABUSED, OR AN ABUSER, OR SOMEONE WHO IS CONCERNED ABOUT ABUSE, I WILL CONSIDER IT A SUCCESS. TO ME, SEEKING MY OWN HEALING, I AM ITS SUCCESS.

♡Amber

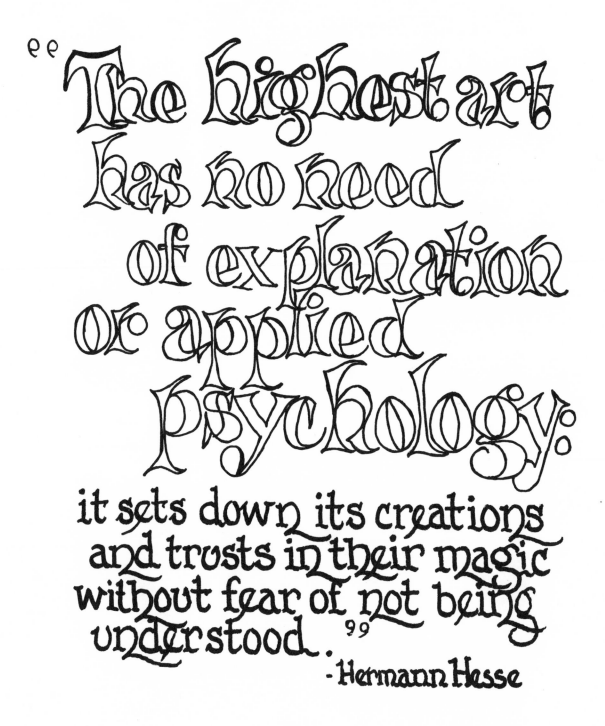

"The highest art
has no need
of explanation
or applied
psychology:
it sets down its creations
and trusts in their magic
without fear of not being
understood. "
— Hermann Hesse

7

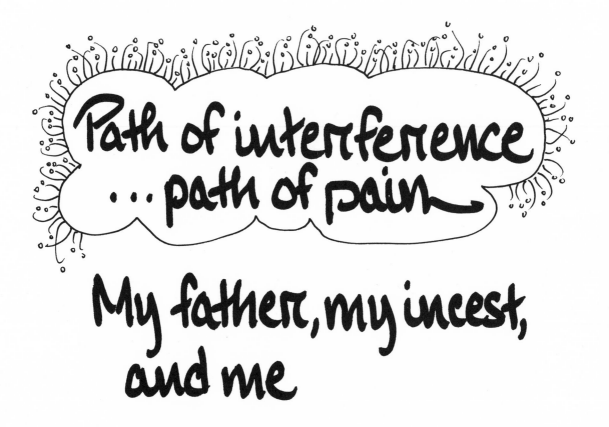

Path of interference ... path of pain

My father, my incest, and me

Dad...

I want you to understand an intense sadness and reality I must deal with every hour of every day of my life...

the acute awareness that if you had not interfered with my life ~ with the process that was rightfully mine... if you had not interfered, I would most probably have had a life quite different than the one I am struggling with today. And I am not so certain about whether I can forgive you that. ~ Amber

I never tolerated well being forced to do anything! My father would force me to remain with him while other members of the family went somewhere. He would not allow me to play with my friends. He would force me to kiss him?

He would force my legs
apart. He ...
—— I cannot finish
this !!! (he would force me
to TOUCH him !!!)

Amber

when
he touched
me... I screamed
at God. Make
oh please, make him stop
Make him stop !!!
(over and over
and over
again

14

Daddy,

understand my love for you. You will never understand my soul's journey. But you will never understand this love, Amber

You will never You do not hear me. You do not see me... To say it simply: i love you... to say it complexly: i love you. understood me. Daddy, come with me on my journey. Do not be afraid, for i will hold you dearly. i will hold you dearly.

Sometimes it included you, sometimes it eluded you.

this love is forgiveness. My love seeks God's understanding.

Please Say You're Sorry...

Daddy, you have never understand this for you will never understand this for you

Here is my song for you ...i shall sing and dance for you so gently you may even smile— you may even cry but i think not...for you will never understand me.

15

Amanda and I had the eternal problem of keeping our room neat and orderly. It was an unusually large room. Perhaps I say this because, at the time, it seemed so large and impossible to clean. I was probably six at the time and Mandy was four.

Dad was extremely angry because we weren't getting the job done. We would stop too many times to play house or other games — anything to divert ourselves from our task.

Well, we went too far. Mother and Dad came into our room and Dad literally threw us on to our respective beds. He then began to gather up our toys and throw them into a box.

"Out to the garbage!" he shouted. He grabbed one of Amanda's favorite toys. She began to protest.

"And you! You little son-of-a-bitch... is this yours?" He picked up one of her tennies. "Here!" he yelled. He threw it at her, hitting her in the face. Blood poured out of her nose and ran down her face.

She began to scream, and I screamed ...but there was only one voice—hers! My screams were always internal. I stifled my cries ~ I did not want him to hurt me too.

Mom told him to leave us alone. She

rushed over to comfort Mandy. She was very angry. He went away— but not without our toys. How devastating.

It was a good thing that I happened to be playing in the front foyer a few weeks later. I discovered my Baby Doll's arm dangling out of a paper bag on the shelf above the coats...

it was Christmas all over again

i had found the toys!!!

Amber

18

Second Grade

As a child, I rarely had to be disciplined. A look or frown was enough to cut me to the quick. An angry word or two was enough to bring on the tears and, of course, long periods of painful awareness that I was not liked. If anyone touched me in anger, I sobbed for hours... mostly internally. It was always devastating.

I remember one particular incident that happened in second grade. My teacher,

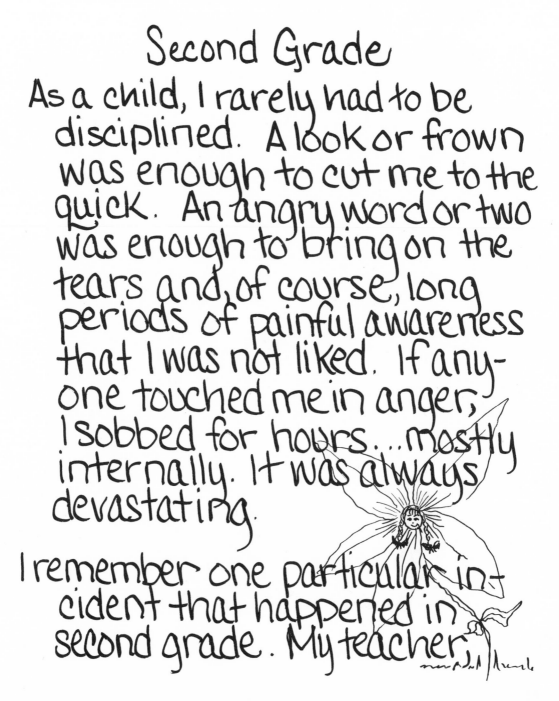

Sister Mora, had a strong dislike for me and displayed this on many occasions, always in an act to humiliate me in front of my classmates.

I had missed school the previous day. Sister Mora had me go to the blackboard to work a subtraction problem. As I had not been in school the day before, I did not know how to work the problem. She grabbed my braids and slammed my head against the blackboard. I remember my face slapping against the cold slate.

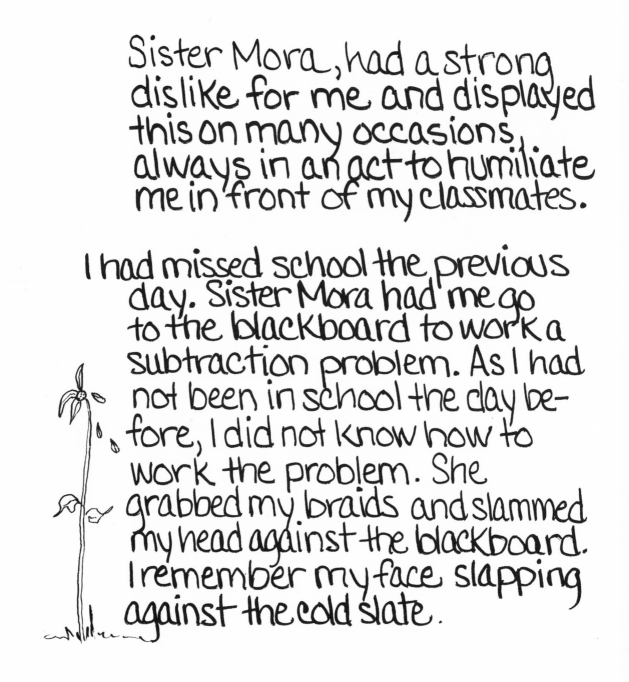

Although I was screaming inside, it was not from the pain, but from my deep humiliation at this violent act.

I sank to my knees with my face turned to the wall. I did not want anyone to see me. Naturally, I could not hold back the tears.

I remember looking at the water-colors we had done for art, now propped against the wall under the blackboard, and watching in horror as my tears splashed on the art work and made the colors run.

I had a horrible, sick feeling because I knew, without a doubt, that they, the artists, would be upset with me for ruining their art work. I was always thinking the worst and having very uncomfortable thoughts about everything. I often felt like throwing up.

Mother Mary,
pray for me
and all the
children
of
the
world.

i prayed so many times
to my guardian angel
to help me
—she never answered...
i truly believed god
forgot to give me
a guardian angel
...such a feeling of
complete helplessness...

Why is it my cloud
has all the moss??

Susan was my best friend when I was seven. She was the smartest one in my class... and the prettiest. She took special care of me... protecting me from those who were mean. Susan was elected to be princess at the p.t.a. carnival only She got sick and couldn't go. She told our teacher that because i could fit into her dress, i should go as princess. Sister Mora only glared at me and said no. I loved Susan... she was my adopted guardian angel.

Susan

♡Amber

Cornered Again

i remember one particular day...
my father was talking to me in the
corner of the kitchen. He was
speaking very softly and quite low.
He was describing in detail what
"we" were going to do that afternoon.
My mother was going to take my
older brother and younger sister
somewhere.

i was "frozen" in a physical and
emotional state of fear...i could
not move. My mother
entered the room and be-
came upset. She demanded
to know what was wrong
with me. My father, in
a gruff voice, said, "Leave
her alone. She's always
like that." Then he
walked away.
                            -Amber

Out in the open, I did not feel so trapped...so alone~out among the daisies and forget-me-nots.

Amber

28

The Princess

The very first moment I remember thinking of myself as a princess is when I was six years old. I remember this because much was being said about Queen Elizabeth, who had just been crowned Queen of England. There was talk also of young Prince Charles. There was little doubt in my mind that someday he would find me and take me away.

When Prince Charles married Lady Diana, my heart nearly broke. It's amazing how reality can come at you all at once.

Amber...there's no one like me.

Memories of 1953

During my first year at St. Joseph's, when I was seven years old, I rarely played with my classmates at recess. I could be found huddled in a corner of the playground, watching silently, arms wrapped tightly around my knees, and waiting for the bell to ring.

On one particular day, I ventured from my corner because of the kind encouragement of a classmate. Soon I found myself enthusiastically swinging among the "giants." The "giants" consisted of several chains with large rings on the ends. Grasping a ring, I began joyously swinging 'round and 'round, pushed ever so wonderfully by the same classmate who had coaxed me to play. It was charmingly exhilarating.

On this same day, I was wearing a not-so-favorite pair of underpants. As fate would have it, the elastic separated itself from the cotton and my panties were flung to the wind. I remember glancing over my shoulder and seeing them hurtling through the air. I longed for my corner, so that I could bury my head and ignore the world once again.

Needless to say, the overwhelming humiliation was enough to render me paralyzed. This paralysis seemed to last several weeks, although measured in everyday reality it was probably only 15 minutes. As could be expected, I was taunted, prodded and poked. My new found confidence faded within my meager being.

               —Amber

And Other Sacred Cows

Sister Mora gave my fellow class-mates and me the alarm-ing news:

    1. there was no Easter Bunny...

    2. there was no Tooth Fairy...

    3. there was no Santa!

Why she should have taken upon herself the task of slapping "reality" to all the seven-year-olds in her path has always escaped me.

The realization of these newly discovered "truths"

affected me in a most traumatic way. I could talk to no one about it ~ not even my mother and father. I thought about it alot.

I remember the day clearly... I was in church one Sunday soon after Sister Mora's magical proclamation. 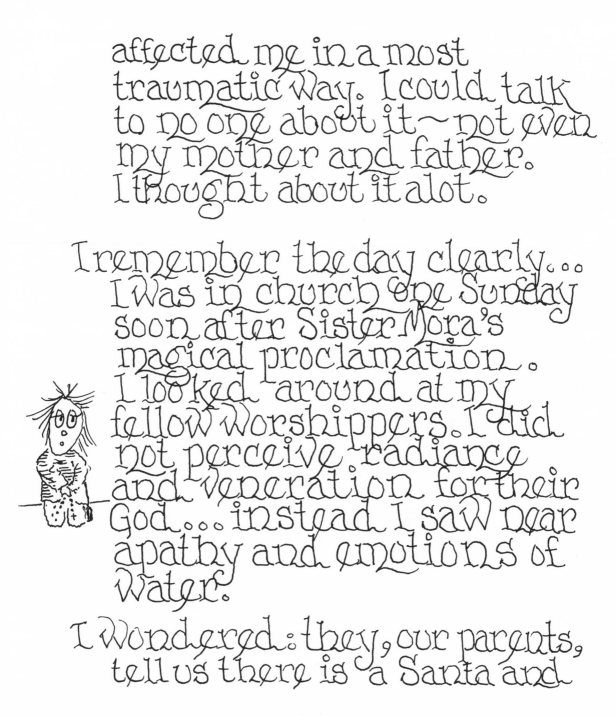 I looked around at my fellow worshippers. I did not perceive radiance and veneration for their God... instead I saw near apathy and emotions of water.

I wondered: they, our parents, tell us there is a Santa and

to be good so that We can
be rewarded....the same
With the Tooth Fairy and
the Easter Bunny.

And how old, I asked
myself,
    how old
        Will i be
        before
    they tell me
        there
            is
            no
                God?

♡♡♡♡♡ AMANDA ♡♡♡♡♡

ON ONE WARM, SUMMER DAY, MY
SISTER, AMANDA, WHO WAS
TWO YEARS YOUNGER THAN
ME, AND I VENTURED ACROSS
THE BUSY AVENUE IN FRONT OF
OUR HOUSE. WE FOUND COTY, OUR
OLDER BROTHER, AND HIS PLAY-
MATES DOWN BY THE CREEK—
THE CREEK WITH ITS ALL-TOO-
RAPID, MOVING WATER. THEY
HAD PLACED A BOARD ACROSS
THE WATER FROM ONE SIDE TO
THE OTHER.

I BECAME VERY FRIGHTENED AND REFUSED TO CROSS THE PLANK.

AMANDA WAS FEARLESS AND BEGAN HER JOURNEY.

NEARLY HALFWAY THERE, SHE LOST HER BALANCE AND TUMBLED INTO THE RIVER. SHE WENT UNDER SEVERAL TIMES, AND THE CURRENT JUST SEEMED TO TAKE HER AWAY. THERE WERE SCREAMS ... AMANDA'S MUFFLED AND FULL OF FEAR ... AND MINE, FULL OF PANIC AND A SENSE OF DOOM! FINALLY, AFTER WHAT SEEMED AN ETERNITY, COTY AND HIS FRIENDS MANAGED TO PULL HER OUT OF THE STREAM. SHE WAS COLD, WET, AND VERY PALE.

IT WAS A LONG WALK BACK TO THE
HOUSE — THE HOUSE THAT RESTED
ON TOP OF THE HILL ON THE ACRE
OF LAND THAT OVERLOOKED
WOODLAND AVENUE. THAT
HILL WAS LIKE A MOUNTAIN TO
CLIMB THAT DAY. I DON'T
BELIEVE I LET GO OF MY SISTER'S
HAND AGAIN ALL DURING THAT
WARM, SUMMER AFTERNOON.

SO MANY TIMES IN MY YOUNG
LIFE I WANTED TO BE HELD
IN A GENTLE, LOVING MANNER.

I WAS ALWAYS AFRAID TO CRY.
I WOULD HAVE MANY MOMENTS
OF SOBBING OR WEEPING AND
MY FRIENDS WOULD NOT
HESITATE TO TAUNT ME AND
CALL ME "CRY BABY"!

I HAVE OFTEN FELT AND I STILL
FEEL THAT IF I ALLOWED MY-
SELF THE LUXURY TO CRY IT
ALL OUT, I WOULD PROBABLY
CRY FOR YEARS... PERHAPS
THIS IS WHY I NEVER ALLOWED
ANYONE TO COME VERY NEAR
TO ME.

Amber Su

Becoming the Storm

There were some very beautiful times living in that old Victorian house on top of the hill.

This may be difficult to comprehend, but my father was, and still is, a very generous man.

We had a porch that wrapped around the entire front of the house.

On warm summer nights, when a storm of thunder and lightning was nearing, Dad would gather us children up in his arms and bring us out to the porch and tuck us gently into the various chairs and divans.

Together, as a family, we would partake in the storm and often enjoy it to its end. We would talk, laugh, and Dad would entertain us with many of his funny stories.

Afterwards Dad would carry us back

upstairs and very gently tuck us into our respective beds.

There are many "sides" to my father. Most of them are probably very good. I just happened to know a side of him that was not.

A QUESTION OF MORALS

During the summer of my 7th year, I began my studies for my First Communion. It was then that I became acutely aware that there had been wrong doing in my life... such wrongs that my soul was probably so black with sin that it would take a great deal of effort on my part in confession to cleanse it, to prepare me for receiving Jesus into my heart and soul in the form of that little white disc.

I completed my studies and, on the Saturday before Communion Sunday, I was to enter the confessional to cleanse myself. Needless to say, I did not sleep or eat well. I stood at the end of the line and allowed everyone to go ahead of me. Finally there was no one left, so I went in.

I had no idea what to say or how to say it. And so, as it turned out, I said nothing. The whole ordeal was a mockery. I mumbled off some half-truths about stealing and not obeying my parents, and, after receiving my penance, I left the confessional and entered the last pew to do my talking to God.

The silence was overwhelming—

and I am not talking about the
absence of sound in the chapel.
I'm talking about the silence in
my soul — not even a whisper.
It was the beginning — the
beginning of my sadness, of
my inner turmoil, of my
frustration, of my anger,
of my denial... of my God.

I did not feel well at all. And if I thought
that particular day was bad,
the next day was horrendous
and so emotionally uncomfortable that it brought about
physical pain. When the host
was presented to me and I
received it on my tongue, I

perceived an acidic, burning sensation.

All of this began my journey down the path toward the imprisonment of my mind and soul. As far as I was concerned, God was locking me away from Himself and throwing away the key... All of this because I could not confess the overwhelming sin of my life. Surely there would be no room for someone like me in the Garden — the Garden where Jesus sits with all the beautiful children at his feet. I would always be in the shadows, wanting to be accepted and so very close to Him... but never asked to come near.

As tears of sunlight surrounded her.

she
proceeded
down
the aisle
toward
God

and sealing
her fate...

Amber~

45

Fears of the Night

When I was 13, Mom had to go to
Salt Lake. Her father was dying,
and she wanted to be there with
her family. She placed me in
charge and tried to teach me
how to use the washer and dryer.
I didn't want her to go. I was in
a constant state of panic about
how Dad would behave.

Amanda and I slept in a double bed.
One night Dad came in and
crawled in between Amanda
and me. First he messed around
with me. Then he turned to
Amanda. I felt nauseated. I pulled
him away from her. He must
have thought I wanted more.
I wanted him dead. I wanted him to
go away. I felt so sick!!

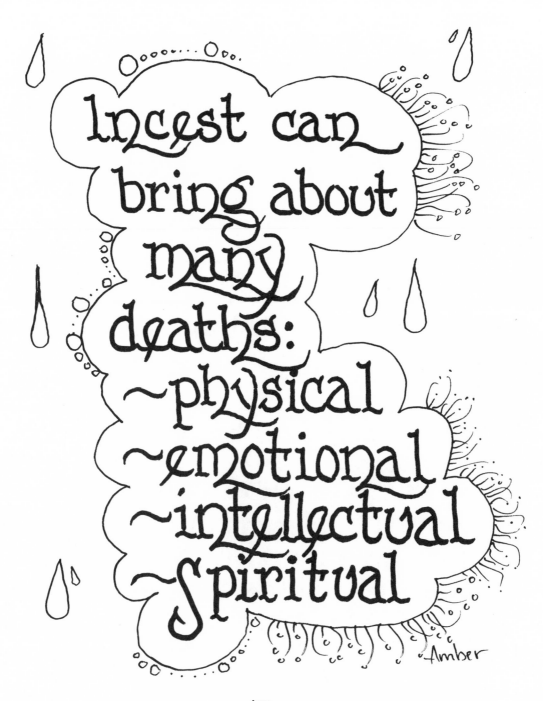

Incest can bring about many deaths:
~physical
~emotional
~intellectual
~spiritual

~Amber

A MATTER OF DEFIANCE

During the summer of my 13th year, I boldly and openly ended my incestuous relationship with my father. Again, no one was home. Again, he approached me. He began touching me. I pulled back and abruptly screamed, "NO! NO MORE!"

I ran from the house, sobbing, I had never defied my father in my life. I sat out in the middle of the lawn, with my knees drawn up to my chest and my arms clamped firmly around them, determined never to let go.

"OH, GOD!" I prayed, "PLEASE HELP ME!"

He came over to me and angrily said, "Get into the house!"

I held onto my knees fiercly. I knew there was no going back. "NO!" I said. "IT IS WRONG! YOU CAN NOT DO THIS TO ME ANYMORE. IT IS AGAINST GOD'S COMMAND- MENT, AND YOU KNOW IT!!"

He then said in a soft voice, "Come on... let's go into the house. We'll talk about it there. Come on." He reached for my arm gently.

"NO!" I said in a low, even, firm voice. "DON'T YOU TOUCH ME... EVER! DON'T YOU EVER TOUCH ME AGAIN.

IF YOU DO I WILL SCREAM AND I WILL CONTINUE TO SCREAM UNTIL SOMEONE COMES TO HELP ME. I AM NOT GOING TO <u>EVER</u> LET YOU TOUCH ME AGAIN."

He walked quietly into the house.

I began to shake... and then the tears came, bringing sweet, gentle release.

OUT IN THE OPEN, I DID
NOT FEEL SO TRAPPED...SO ALONE
~ OUT AMONG THE DAISIES AND
FORGET-ME-NOTS. Amber ♡

Oh Dad, Poor Dad... and i'm feeling so sad.

During my junior year in college, I had taken a course in play directing — a requirement for one of my majors. I had not been doing well in the course... probably because I was gripped with fear at the thought of performing in front of a group of people. I have always disliked having attention drawn to me. In any event, I was not really paying attention to my notes, and, when called on in class for an answer, I rarely had one. I was always preoccupied.

Most of the women in my class (there were only four of us) chose a play they were

familiar with — I was familiar with
none. I had never acted or done back-
stage work in college and very little
during my high school years. Then why
did I select drama as one of my majors?
I have always wanted a well-rounded
background in the creative arts —
and so I ended up with majors in art,
speech, and drama.

The play I selected was <u>Dinny and the Witches</u>.
It was a clear leap into the unknown for
me. It was a clever story about three
old ladies who escaped from a rest home.
They ruled the world as three senile,
old witches. The opening of the play:
"Our Father, who art in Hell..." I
directed the witches to stand over a
caldron — a large garbage can.

I had my father in mind, as I directed
my little play. I knew he would enjoy
the colorful scenery that I designed,
the costumes, the acting — everything.

I was a horrible grouch to work with as the night of our performance neared. The play became all-consuming — how I loved it!

The night of the play, I was so nervous I could barely walk. I kept worrying about whether he would like it.

I didn't have to worry for long... he didn't come. My sister, Amanda, and my mother came. They enjoyed the play, and it really was successful. But!... HE DIDN'T COME! The beautiful roses I received from the cast and the "A" grade I got for the play... these did help compensate, but, dammit, he didn't come.

"OUR FATHER, WHO ART IN HELL..."

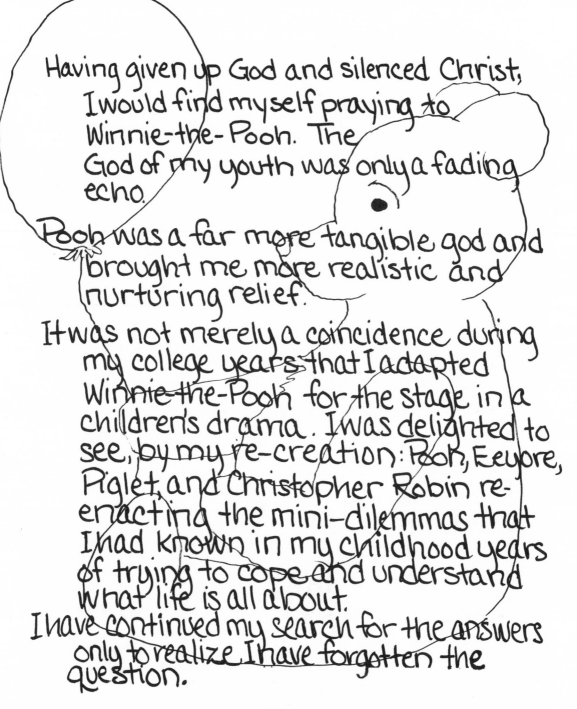

Having given up God and silenced Christ,
  I would find myself praying to
  Winnie-the-Pooh. The
  God of my youth was only a fading
  echo.

Pooh was a far more tangible god and
  brought me more realistic and
  nurturing relief.

It was not merely a coincidence during
  my college years that I adapted
  Winnie-the-Pooh for the stage in a
  children's drama. I was delighted to
  see, by my re-creation: Pooh, Eeyore,
  Piglet, and Christopher Robin re-
  enacting the mini-dilemmas that
  I had known in my childhood years
  of trying to cope and understand
  what life is all about.
I have continued my search for the answers
  only to realize I have forgotten the
  question.

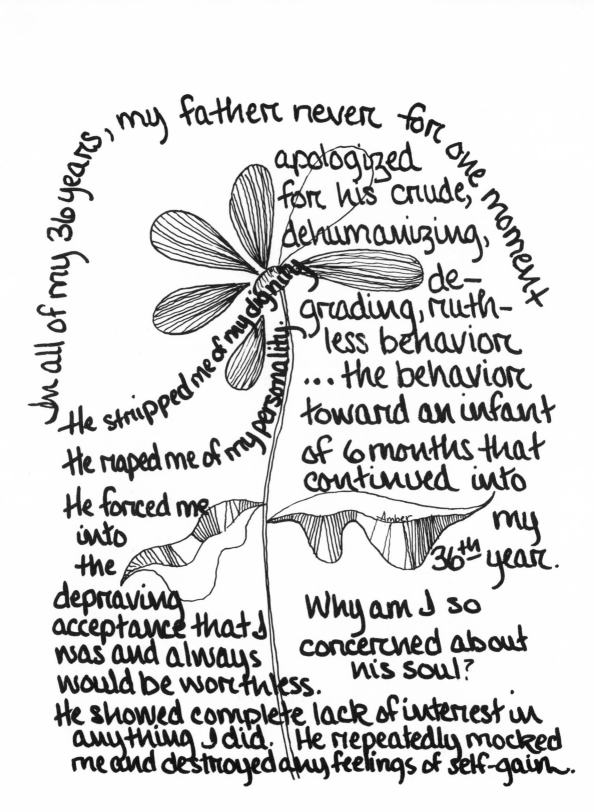

In all of my 36 years, my father never for one moment apologized for his crude, dehumanizing, de-grading, ruth-less behavior ... the behavior toward an infant of 6 months that continued into my 36th year.

He stripped me of my dignity.

He raped me of my personality.

He forced me into the depraving acceptance that I was and always would be worthless.

Why am I so concerned about his soul?

He showed complete lack of interest in anything I did. He repeatedly mocked me and destroyed any feelings of self-gain.

Amber

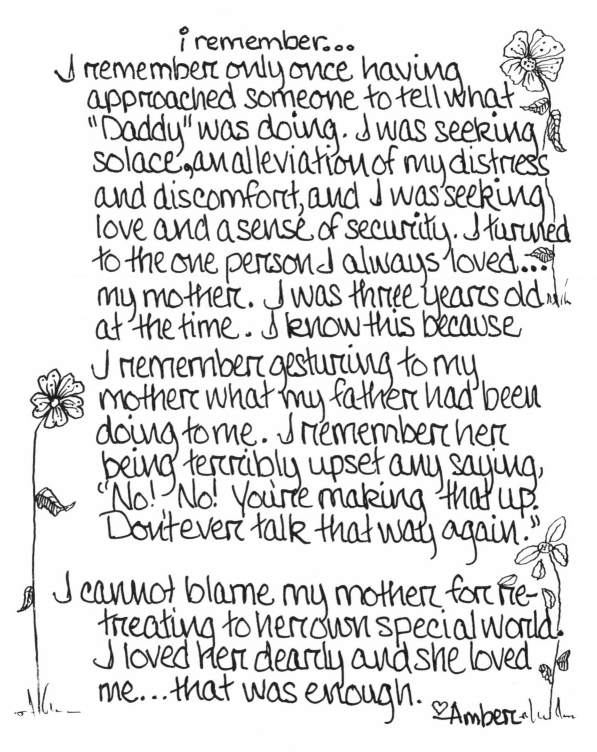

i remember...

I remember only once having approached someone to tell what "Daddy" was doing. I was seeking solace, an alleviation of my distress and discomfort, and I was seeking love and a sense of security. I turned to the one person I always loved... my mother. I was three years old at the time. I know this because

I remember gesturing to my mother what my father had been doing to me. I remember her being terribly upset and saying, "No! No! You're making that up. Don't ever talk that way again."

I cannot blame my mother for retreating to her own special world. I loved her dearly and she loved me... that was enough.

♡Amber

Love and Anger

There were times when I was angry at my mother. Most of the time I did not understand the source of that rage. This, of course, made for very frustrating moments.

I understand now that my anger was based on my sense of abandonment in my childhood. She could have stepped in — she could have interfered with the incestuous relationship I had with my father. She could have spared me years of trauma and pain. She could have done all this, but she did not. When I was 24 years old, at the time of my breakdown, she validated her awareness of "something" going on.

Yes, I experienced the anger. I have examined it. And I have let it go.

My mother was a special lady, a good friend and companion. What she may have gone through, I will never know. I only know I love her dearly in death as in life.

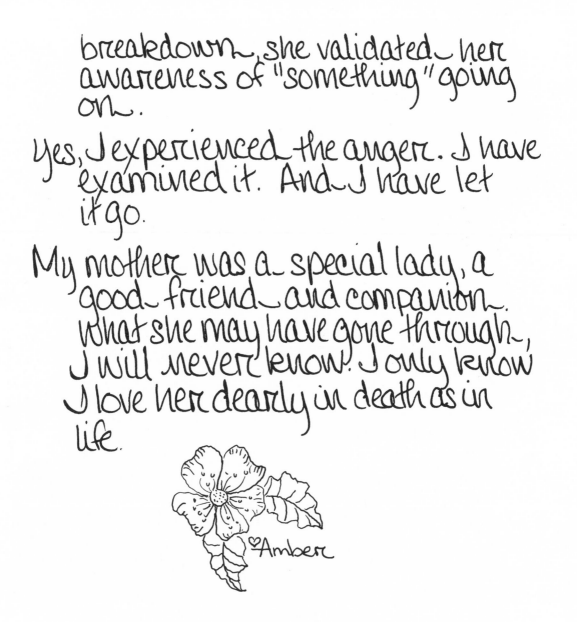

♡Amber

Dennis and Me

i have loved Dennis since 5th grade. i am not the only one. Nearly all the girls fell in love with him. But I got him... in every way, shape, and form. He nearly died because of me. And i loved him dearly even then.

And now, when we are older, we are closer and dearer than we have ever been before. He means so very much to me, and i want to be there for him, just as he has been there for me ... always.

i may decide to marry some-day — so may Dennis. But i don't think so. He's not the marrying kind. No matter what, we will always be close and loving and the best of friends. i think we are brother and sister soul mates, or something like that. Amber

HOW TO KILL YOUR MOTHER
...in one easy lesson

I remember as a very small child listening to my father saying in our all-alone time, "You must never tell your Mother about what you and I are doing. It would kill her."

Of course, I never fully understood what he meant... I believed it meant Mom would die instantly upon impact of the knowledge that Daddy and I were doing something "dirty."

The thought alone of that ever happening stopped me from telling anyone, and, in particular, my mother.

I'll never forget the moment I did tell her... nearly twenty years later. It is as if I killed her by driving the all-too-sharp knife of reality into her very heart and soul... and I am certain it was the beginning of the death of her mind — the slow death that brought her to a state of nonexistence in the nursing home so far away...

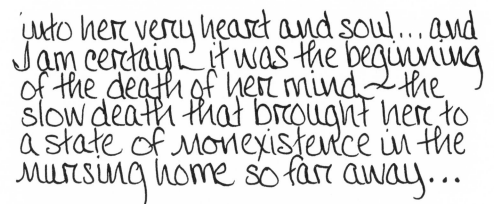

After my breakdown during my teaching years, I returned home on my doctors' advice, to deal with my problems.

Once again, I was alone with my father. He was very upset that I had told anyone anything. This was to be the beginning of his cruel remarks directed only to me. They continue to this day.

At this time I asked him when it all began. After he said I was six months old, I told him Mom had to be told.

He said, "Leave her out of this! I've already discussed this with her!"

"When?" I asked, "When did you tell her?"

"Last night." he said, "There's no use upsetting her further."

That ended our conversation.

A few nights later my mother and I on our nightly walk after dinner, came upon the subject of my breakdown. She asked me what caused it. She said I was such a strong girl—what could have caused such a disastrous happening in my life?

I looked at her... her childlike eyes filled with questioning and doubt.

Was it my imagination or was the screaming reality about to make my nightmarish fear for her come true? Had she simply blocked it out? She was such a gentle soul — so fragile.

Quietly, I began to explain my life long incestuous relationship with my father. How can one be delicate about such stuff.

I barely got into our discussion — and she looked at me with those wide eyes filled with fear, terror, and pain. "What are you saying? What do you mean? With your father? With him?"

I knew at that instant that he had never told her... he had lied. I was telling her for the first time. He lied to me! She never knew! God! I wanted to die...

She looked away for a moment. "Mom," I said, feeling myself fill with pain and tears and absorbing her sorrow and pain... "I'm so sorry. I thought you knew. Dad told me he'd discussed it with you... Oh, Mom!"

I embraced her and sobbed. Both our bodies shook. It was as if our souls were melting into one.

She looked at me... and said, "Oh, Honey, I knew..."—and in a small voice, barely audible, "I knew something was wrong."

There was more than one death that

68

night. I recovered, but I truly do not think she ever did.

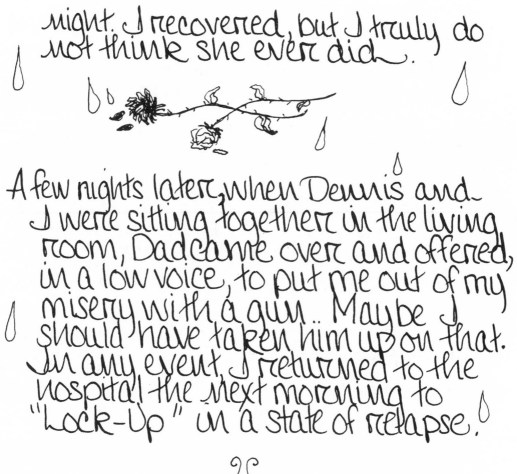

A few nights later, when Dennis and I were sitting together in the living room, Dad came over and offered, in a low voice, to put me out of my misery with a gun. Maybe I should have taken him up on that. In any event, I returned to the hospital the next morning to "Lock-Up" in a state of relapse.

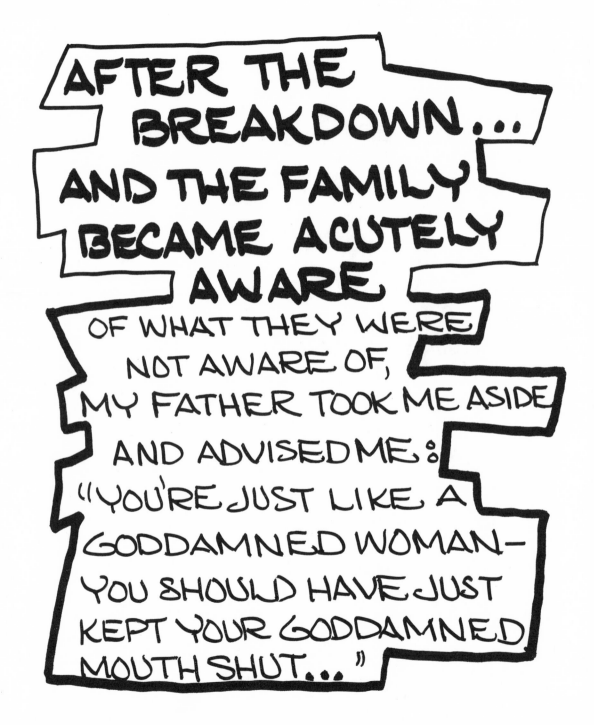

AFTER THE BREAKDOWN... AND THE FAMILY BECAME ACUTELY AWARE OF WHAT THEY WERE NOT AWARE OF, MY FATHER TOOK ME ASIDE AND ADVISED ME: "YOU'RE JUST LIKE A GODDAMNED WOMAN—YOU SHOULD HAVE JUST KEPT YOUR GODDAMNED MOUTH SHUT..."

DEATH AT TWENTY-FOUR

When I was twenty-four years old
and it was all out in the open ~
at least with my family ~ I had
to somehow tell Dennis.

Two minutes after I told him, I knew
in my heart our love relationship
was over. He couldn't bear it.
He just wept.

Afterwards he looked at me and
said, "I hate your father. I will
never forgive him."

Then he looked away. He never
looked at me in the same light
again. The pain I experienced
that night was immeasurable.
I shall never forget it.

My father believes
he had the 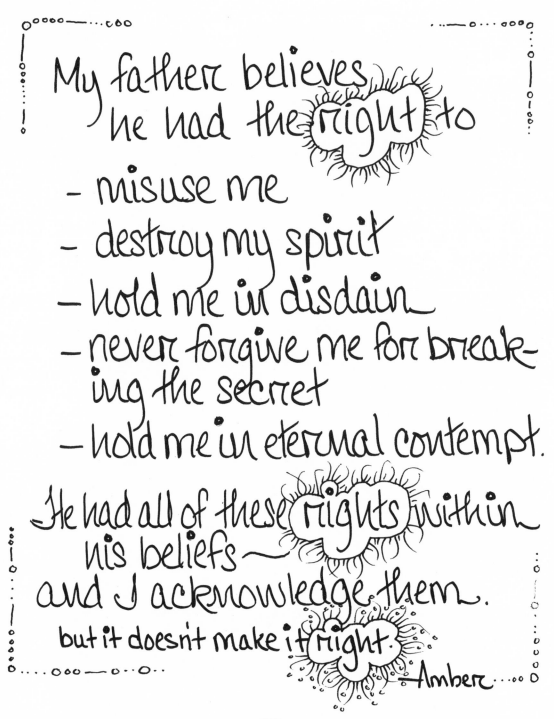 right to

- misuse me
- destroy my spirit
- hold me in disdain
- never forgive me for breaking the secret
- hold me in eternal contempt.

He had all of these rights within
his beliefs —
and I acknowledge them.
but it doesn't make it right.

— Amber

Save this tear for me...

i never
Want
to
forget.

—Amber

My mother suffered from Alzheimer's disease. It affects the body in many disarming ways. It was diagnosed in 1976. And for eight years she resided in a nursing home in another state. Toward the end her mind seemed to be completely gone.

On my visits, to be with her, I just sat by her and looked into her childlike, vacant eyes and wondered what was still there. As I sat beside her, just loving her and all that she had been, I was thankful that she was not in any apparent pain. That lady meant more to me than any other living soul. The beautiful and close moments we shared will be with me always.   ♡Amber

A COUPLE OF YEARS AGO I WENT
TO SEE MY FATHER AND MOTHER.
MY MOTHER WAS IN A NURSING
HOME THREE BLOCKS AWAY
FROM MY FATHER'S HOUSE.

ONE EVENING MY FATHER SAID,
"I GUESS WHAT I DID TO YOU
AS A KID WAS WRONG..."

I THOUGHT THIS WAS TO BE AN
APOLOGY. I WAS MISTAKEN.

"WELL," HE CONTINUED, "IT'S NOT
WRONG NOW THAT YOU'RE OLDER.
LET'S GO INTO THE BEDROOM AND
HAVE SEX."

THAT MAN WILL NEVER CEASE TO
AMAZE ME, TO SHOCK ME, AND
TO HURT ME. MY REACTION WAS
EMBARASSMENT, ANGER, AND
A FLASHBACK OF ALL THE BAD
EXPERIENCES OF MY PAST. I TOLD
HIM TO GO TO HELL!

Here's a little drawing for you, Mom.
I hope today brings you more joy than
yesterday and less sorrow than
tomorrow.

Mom,
Hello — you know I miss you so much
...your good humor, your company,

your twinkling eyes. I want to communicate with you in the best possible way. This is why I am writing this book.

If you cannot be here with me and I cannot be with you, then I will regress a little. I will go back to the years of my childhood when I communicated my best (and worst) feelings by my drawings and secret writings.

This is just for you, Mom, because I love you so much. You may never see my book but, God knows, you are aware of it. I love you, Amber

The beautiful and close moments
we've shared will never
perish from my mind.
Amber 1983

Your soul will always soar
much higher and freer
than mine.

Mother Mary
1914–1984

in the depth of your hopes and desires lies your silent knowledge of the beyond; and like seeds dreaming beneath the snow your heart dreams of spring...trust the dreams for in them is hidden the gate to eternity....

Kahil gibran ~ THE PROPHET

Amber

Path to Enlightenment
... path of sorrows

My mental illness

The Violence Within

My family had such violent arguments,
as I experienced them, although
not a single blow was struck.
I reacted with tears and shaking.
Near the end of the storm there
was always laughter - twisted
and insane. I couldn't take it.
I thought I was going to crack up.
One day I did. Why is it that
my sanity - or insanity - was
taken so lightly? I had enemies
within my family. I grew to
hate them — those who abused
me so.

—Amber

ABUSED AT SIX MONTHS...

MY ABUSE BEGAN WHEN I WAS SIX MONTHS OLD. THIS BECAME KNOWN TO ME WHEN I ASKED MY FATHER ABOUT IT AFTER MY "ENLIGHT-ENING" BREAKDOWN DURING MY SECOND YEAR OF TEACHING.

BOLDLY I ASKED WHEN IT BEGAN. AFTER HE TOLD ME I WAS SIX MONTHS OLD, HE LAVISHLY DESCRIBED IN GRAPHIC DETAIL WHAT A MAN COULD DO TO A BABY OF SIX MONTHS. I FELT SO NAUSEOUS AND REVILED! IT WILL BURN IN MY MEMORY, PERHAPS FOR ETERNITY, AND YET I CAN-NOT TELL YOU EXACTLY WHAT HE DID. THERE IS LITTLE DOUBT IN MY MIND THAT HE WAS SOMEWHAT MAD.

Why Did You Do This to Me, Daddy?

I ASKED HIM "WHY?"
AND, "HOW COULD YOU
DO THIS TO AN
INNOCENT... TO A
CHILD?"

He replied, "For two reasons:
One — you were a beautiful
child;
Two — I am a Man!"
"Besides," he continued, "don't
forget... it was a two-way
street!"
SOMETIMES I JUST DON'T
UNDERSTAND "REASON"!

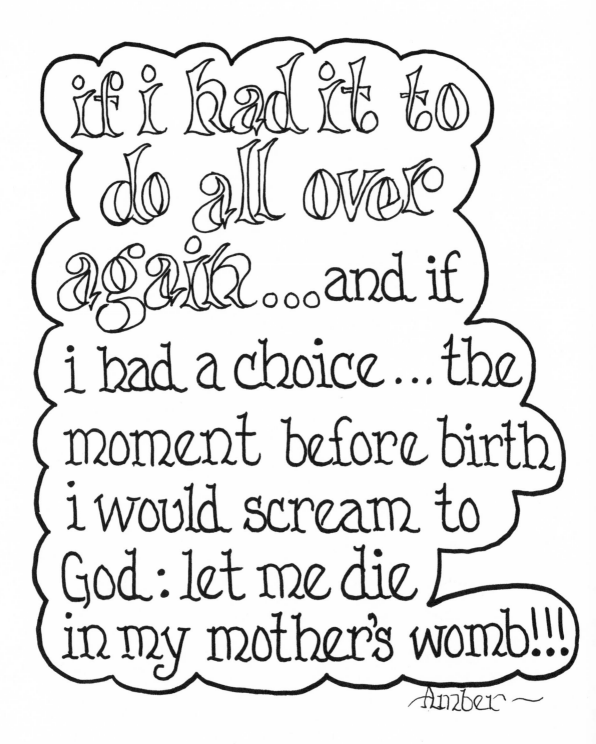

THE VIET NAM WAR WAS HARD ON
A GREAT NUMBER OF US. AS I
WAS MOST DEFINITELY A CHILD
OF THE SIXTIES, THE WAR OPENED
WOUNDS WITHIN MY PSYCHE
THAT HAVE NEVER CLOSED.

THERE WERE ONLY A HANDFUL OF US
AT COLLEGE THAT DID ANY
PROTESTING OUT IN THE OPEN.
THE "RELIGIOUS" OPPOSED US.
I REMEMBER PLACING A POSTER
ON A TABLE BY THE CHAPEL. IT
HAD AN ANTI-WAR THEME. I FOUND
IT FACE DOWN ON THE SPARKLING
CLEAN MARBLE FLOOR, WITH
FOOTPRINTS ALL OVER IT...

IN MARCH OF '75, SEVERAL YEARS

LATER, SAIGON FELL, MARKING
AN OFFICIAL END TO THE WAR.
I DID NOT FEEL RELIEVED OR
JOYOUS. I BECAME VERY ANGRY.
THIS WAS IT... MY FINAL CON-
FRONTATION WITH GOD!

I MARCHED OUT TO THE FROZEN
SHORES OF LAKE SUPERIOR
...WITH ITS ICE PACKED SO
HIGH I HAD TO CLAMBER UP GLASSY
MOUNDS OF ICE. I COULD HOLD
IT IN NO LONGER... MY COMPLETE
DISGUST AT GOD FOR THE MIS-
ERABLE WAY HE HANDLED
THINGS... MY CHILDHOOD AND
HIS ABANDONING ME... MY
BELOVED DENNIS AND HOW HE
HAD BROUGHT COMPLETE RUIN
TO OUR RELATIONSHIP... AND
THIS WAR! THIS COMPLETE
MOCKERY OF A "JUST" WAR.

I SCREAMED, "YOU CALL YOURSELF
GOD AND THIS IS HOW YOU
TREAT HUMANITY. HOW CAN
YOU?" I SHOUTED AS THOUGH
MY LUNGS WOULD COLLAPSE.
"DON'T YOU EVER COME INTO
MY LIFE AGAIN! I AM DONE
WITH YOU. YOU ARE LESS THAN
NOTHING TO ME. GO AWAY!
YOU ARE DEAD! YOU ARE DEAD
BECAUSE I AM KILLING YOU.
I CANNOT STAND YOU ANY
LONGER... GO AWAY!!"

I STOOD THERE WITH TEARS FROZEN
TO MY CHEEKS. MY BODY
SHOOK AND I WANTED TO DIE.
THERE WAS NO GENTLE
RELEASE FROM MY TEARS.
THERE WAS NO FIELD OF
DAISIES OR FORGET-ME-NOTS.

IT WAS TIME FOR GRIEVING AND
SORROW... I FELT AS THOUGH
I HAD LOST A CHILD ~ THE ONE
WITHIN.

IT WAS TIME FOR ME TO
FORGET... AFTER ALL

I HAD JUST KILLED

THE GOD
OF
MY YOUTH.

CLEANING OUT THE COBWEBS

I have dared to go back to the moment of
the original psychotic "break"...
my moment of enlightenment!
My therapists discouraged me from
doing so, as did family members
and friends. It was ultimately
necessary to make such a journey. Something definitely was
taking place, and it seemed to have
little or nothing to do with the
conflicts of my childhood. Instead,
it had a great deal to do with that
obscene war in Viet Nam.

Teaching at a military establishment,
where I was confronted with
sensitive, gentle, and delightful
children, without question encouraged my personal conflicts

with war.

During the first week of March, 1970,
    I realized the war was indeed
    going to escalate. This being so,
    we were in real trouble here at
    home as well as in Viet Nam.
    I panicked and believed the
    President must be warned of
    this.

Now I have come to realize that my
    innocence and naivety at this
    point were most likely respons-
    ible for my downfall. I truly
    believed I was a "messiah",
    not realizing that the world
    was full of messiahs and that
    our government did not give
    a tinker's damn about the con-
    cerns of a somewhat misguided

"savior of the world".

In a moment of panic I lost it all, gave my mind to the Viet Nam War. That should be enough. It can't happen again. It was far too much to lose and the journey back was sheer hell.

I knew, as many did, that our country was in serious trouble within its cracking confines here at home. That awareness carried with it a guilt that should not have been there. I accepted and believed myself solely respons- ible for every life lost from that first week in March 1970 —whether American, Vietnamese, or Viet Cong. I believed I could have stopped the war but I needed the "right" people to listen to me. The answer to the problem had to do with Love. I did not realize at the time that the World Problems were very similar and reflective of my own personal problems. All of this has brought an intense sadness that all my years of therapy have not touched.

Only recently, at some very fine workshops, I did stand and speak of this particular pain. I have forgiven myself my innocence. I cannot say the same for my country.

— Amber

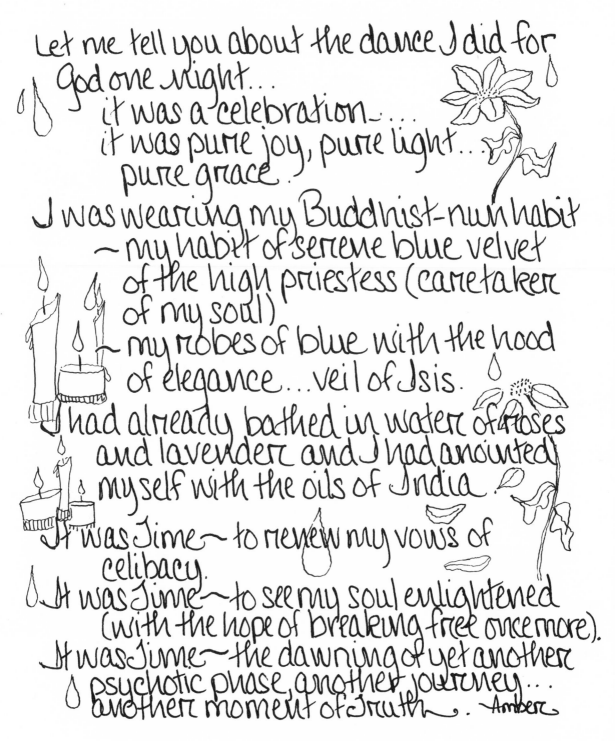

Let me tell you about the dance I did for
God one night...
   it was a celebration....
   it was pure joy, pure light...
   pure grace...

I was wearing my Buddhist-nun habit
   ~ my habit of serene blue velvet
      of the high priestess (caretaker
      of my soul)
   ~ my robes of blue with the hood
      of elegance...veil of Isis.
I had already bathed in water of roses
   and lavender and I had anointed
   myself with the oils of India.

It was Time~ to renew my vows of
   celibacy.
It was Time~ to see my soul enlightened
   (with the hope of breaking free once more).
It was Time~ the dawning of yet another
   psychotic phase, another journey...
   another moment of Truth. —Amber

95

Iris: regarded as goddess of the rainbow bringing color and grandeur.

Amber

The Dance of Life —

DEEP, DEEP WITHIN THE INTRICATE LACE
OF MY PSYCHOSIS THERE IS A PLACE
WHERE I DWELL. IT IS GOOD THERE.
I AM SAFE. I AM WARM. I SMILE AS
THE RECLINING BUDDHA — THE ALL-
KNOWING BUDDHA — AND, AS I DREAM,
THERE ARE GENTLE TIGER LILIES,
BLUE BUTTERFLIES, AND COBRAS OF
PINK CRYSTAL. THE AIR IS FRESH
AND CRISP AND I HAVE ONLY TO FLUTTER
MY EYES AND THE MAIDENS OF
SPRING SURROUND ME. I AM PRO-
TECTED. I AM BEAUTIFUL. I AM
WITHOUT PAIN.

There are moments within my everyday
happenings that I choose to return to
the land of the crystal cobras and
sleeping Buddhas. Without having
experienced the psychosis of my manic
phases, I might never have known
such serene tranquility, such pure
joy and light... such a closeness to
God.
♡ Amber

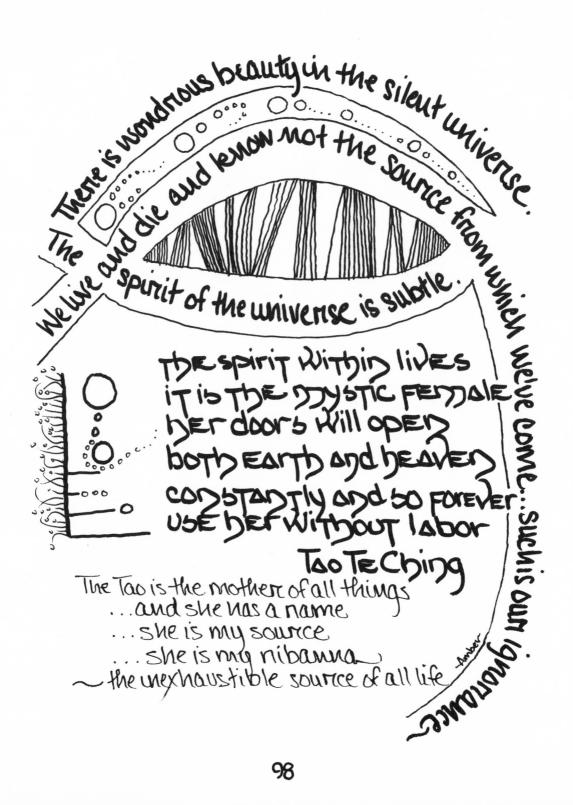

There is wondrous beauty in the silent universe.

The We live and die and know not the source from which we've come...Such is our ignorance.

spirit of the universe is subtle.

The spirit within lives
it is the mystic female
her doors will open
both earth and heaven
constantly and so forever
use her without labor

Tao Te Ching

The Tao is the mother of all things
...and she has a name
...she is my source
...she is my nibanna
~ the unexhaustible source of all life

Amber

LOCK-UP

I had several psychotic episodes. During my manic phases I had to enter the Mental Health unit ...always way in back in "Lock-Up." This, of course, was extremely hard on me. Looking back, I realize these episodes were part of my necessary journey to Enlightenment — toward cleansing my soul.

Back in "Lock-Up," I could act out my frustrations, angers, and intense sadness.

These phases were hard on my family and close friends. My father's attitude was blunt: Give her a swift kick in the ass and she'll be all right! Then

he would turn his back on me
... he never contacted me by
phone or mail or visited me.
I really was not surprised.

Coty's wife, Judy, became very
close to me throughout my
mental illness. She allowed me
to cry, to laugh, to hurt and
never scolded me for "un=
appropriate" behavior. I love
her dearly to this day... she
is like a soul-sister.

Dennis was and is always there,
no matter what phase our
relationship has been in. He
has brought such clarity
and healthy-insane humor
to my troubled times.

My mother drove down to see me nearly every other day. She always stopped at the green house at the edge of town and purchased a flower... always a rose and always in a different hue. She sent me cards every day... such a fine lady, such a comfort, such a love!

My mother often did things such as this. She didn't need explanations. She just loved me without judging, without criticism. I wanted so much to be like her.

Amber

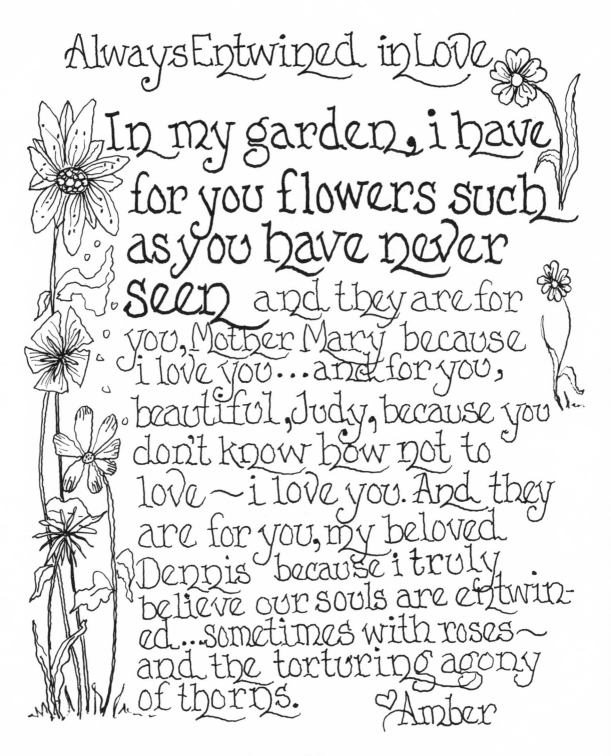

Always Entwined in Love

In my garden, i have for you flowers such as you have never seen and they are for you, Mother Mary because i love you...and for you, beautiful, Judy, because you don't know how not to love ~ i love you. And they are for you, my beloved Dennis because i truly believe our souls are entwined...sometimes with roses ~ and the torturing agony of thorns.
♡Amber

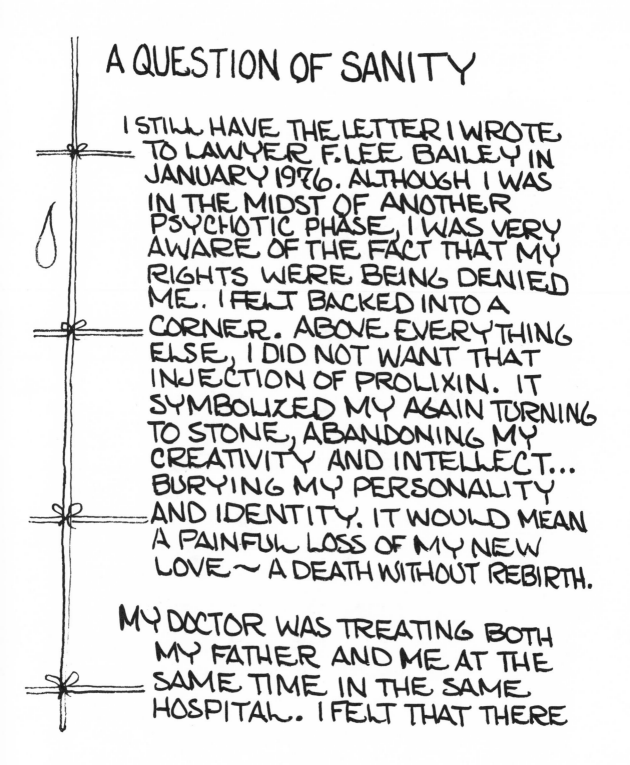

A QUESTION OF SANITY

I STILL HAVE THE LETTER I WROTE TO LAWYER F. LEE BAILEY IN JANUARY 1976. ALTHOUGH I WAS IN THE MIDST OF ANOTHER PSYCHOTIC PHASE, I WAS VERY AWARE OF THE FACT THAT MY RIGHTS WERE BEING DENIED ME. I FELT BACKED INTO A CORNER. ABOVE EVERYTHING ELSE, I DID NOT WANT THAT INJECTION OF PROLIXIN. IT SYMBOLIZED MY AGAIN TURNING TO STONE, ABANDONING MY CREATIVITY AND INTELLECT... BURYING MY PERSONALITY AND IDENTITY. IT WOULD MEAN A PAINFUL LOSS OF MY NEW LOVE ~ A DEATH WITHOUT REBIRTH.

MY DOCTOR WAS TREATING BOTH MY FATHER AND ME AT THE SAME TIME IN THE SAME HOSPITAL. I FELT THAT THERE

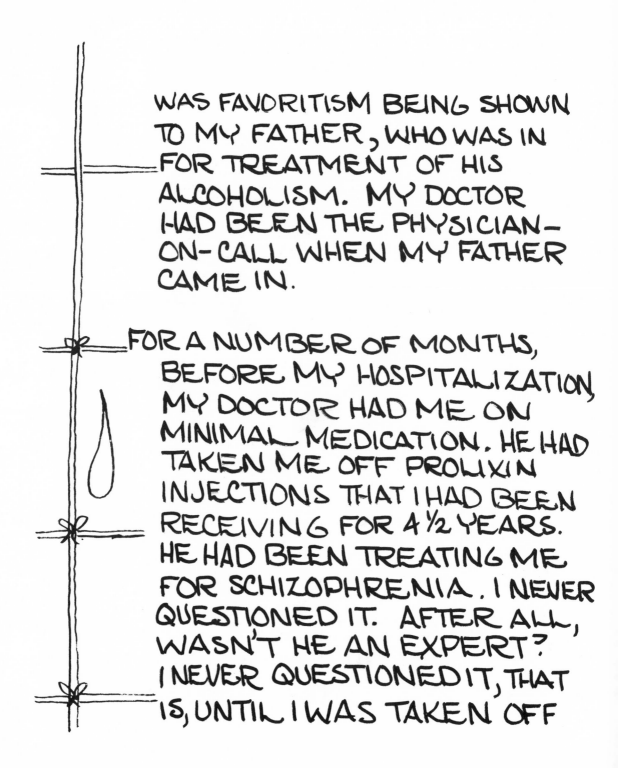

WAS FAVORITISM BEING SHOWN
TO MY FATHER, WHO WAS IN
FOR TREATMENT OF HIS
ALCOHOLISM. MY DOCTOR
HAD BEEN THE PHYSICIAN—
ON-CALL WHEN MY FATHER
CAME IN.

FOR A NUMBER OF MONTHS,
BEFORE MY HOSPITALIZATION,
MY DOCTOR HAD ME ON
MINIMAL MEDICATION. HE HAD
TAKEN ME OFF PROLIXIN
INJECTIONS THAT I HAD BEEN
RECEIVING FOR 4½ YEARS.
HE HAD BEEN TREATING ME
FOR SCHIZOPHRENIA. I NEVER
QUESTIONED IT. AFTER ALL,
WASN'T HE AN EXPERT?
I NEVER QUESTIONED IT, THAT
IS, UNTIL I WAS TAKEN OFF

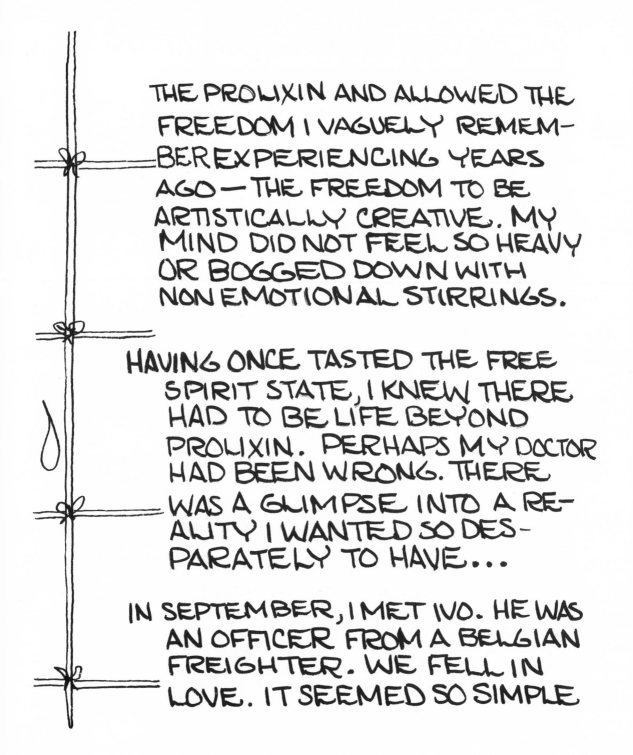

THE PROLIXIN AND ALLOWED THE
FREEDOM I VAGUELY REMEM-
BER EXPERIENCING YEARS
AGO — THE FREEDOM TO BE
ARTISTICALLY CREATIVE. MY
MIND DID NOT FEEL SO HEAVY
OR BOGGED DOWN WITH
NON EMOTIONAL STIRRINGS.

HAVING ONCE TASTED THE FREE
SPIRIT STATE, I KNEW THERE
HAD TO BE LIFE BEYOND
PROLIXIN. PERHAPS MY DOCTOR
HAD BEEN WRONG. THERE
WAS A GLIMPSE INTO A RE-
ALITY I WANTED SO DES-
PARATELY TO HAVE....

IN SEPTEMBER, I MET IVO. HE WAS
AN OFFICER FROM A BELGIAN
FREIGHTER. WE FELL IN
LOVE. IT SEEMED SO SIMPLE

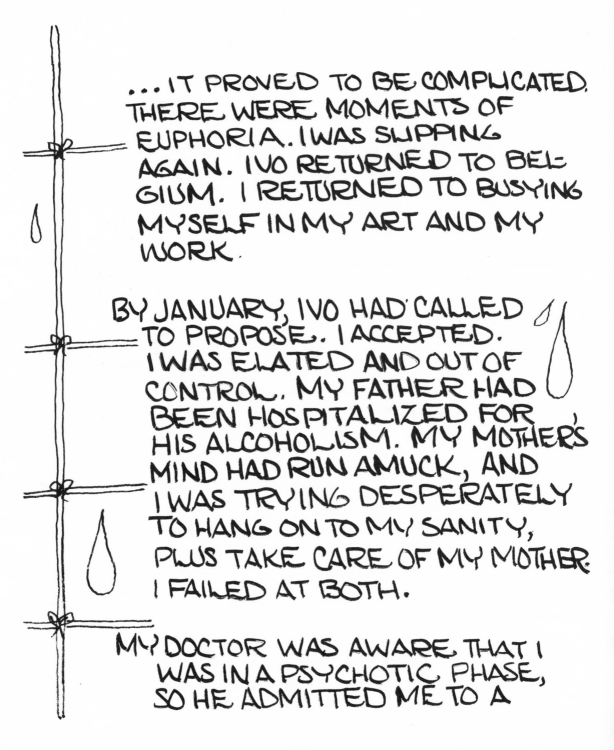

...IT PROVED TO BE COMPLICATED. THERE WERE MOMENTS OF EUPHORIA. I WAS SLIPPING AGAIN. IVO RETURNED TO BELGIUM. I RETURNED TO BUSYING MYSELF IN MY ART AND MY WORK.

BY JANUARY, IVO HAD CALLED TO PROPOSE. I ACCEPTED. I WAS ELATED AND OUT OF CONTROL. MY FATHER HAD BEEN HOSPITALIZED FOR HIS ALCOHOLISM. MY MOTHER'S MIND HAD RUN AMUCK, AND I WAS TRYING DESPERATELY TO HANG ON TO MY SANITY, PLUS TAKE CARE OF MY MOTHER. I FAILED AT BOTH.

MY DOCTOR WAS AWARE THAT I WAS IN A PSYCHOTIC PHASE, SO HE ADMITTED ME TO A

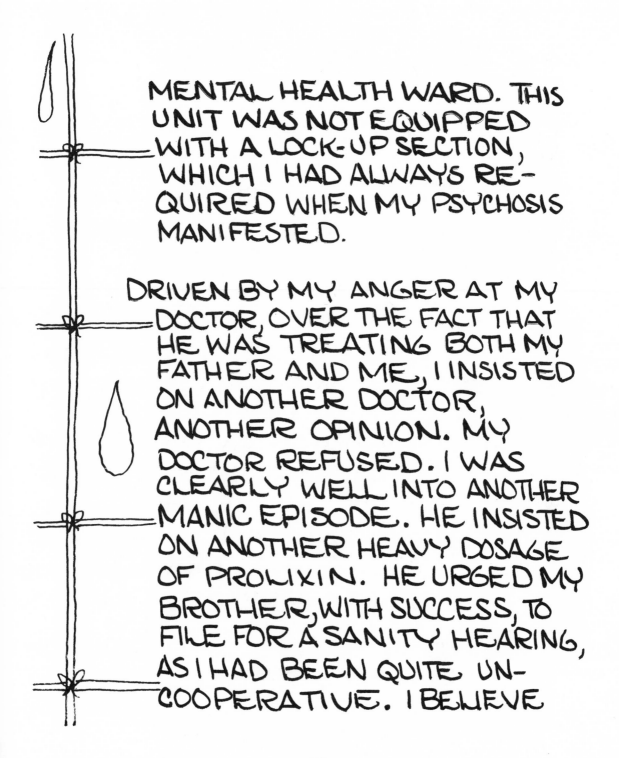

MENTAL HEALTH WARD. THIS
UNIT WAS NOT EQUIPPED
WITH A LOCK-UP SECTION,
WHICH I HAD ALWAYS RE-
QUIRED WHEN MY PSYCHOSIS
MANIFESTED.

DRIVEN BY MY ANGER AT MY
DOCTOR, OVER THE FACT THAT
HE WAS TREATING BOTH MY
FATHER AND ME, I INSISTED
ON ANOTHER DOCTOR,
ANOTHER OPINION. MY
DOCTOR REFUSED. I WAS
CLEARLY WELL INTO ANOTHER
MANIC EPISODE. HE INSISTED
ON ANOTHER HEAVY DOSAGE
OF PROLIXIN. HE URGED MY
BROTHER, WITH SUCCESS, TO
FILE FOR A SANITY HEARING,
AS I HAD BEEN QUITE UN-
COOPERATIVE. I BELIEVE

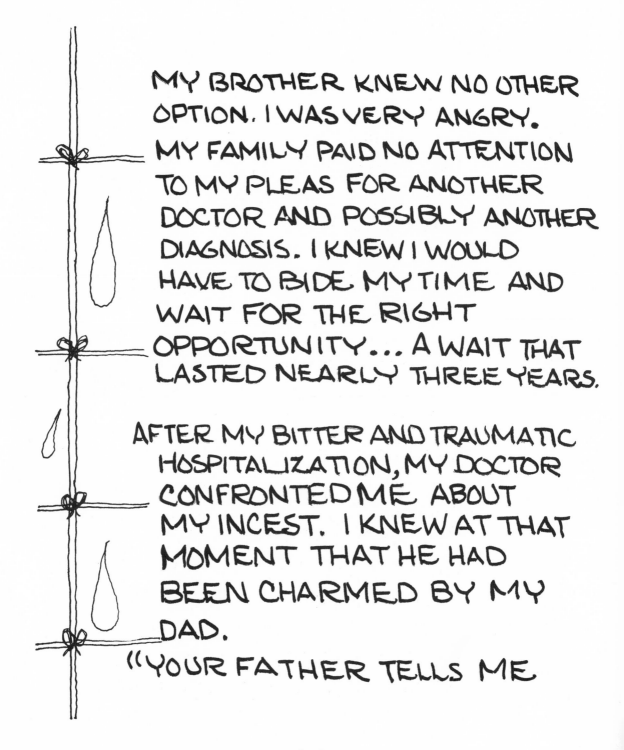

MY BROTHER KNEW NO OTHER
OPTION. I WAS VERY ANGRY.
MY FAMILY PAID NO ATTENTION
TO MY PLEAS FOR ANOTHER
DOCTOR AND POSSIBLY ANOTHER
DIAGNOSIS. I KNEW I WOULD
HAVE TO BIDE MY TIME AND
WAIT FOR THE RIGHT
OPPORTUNITY... A WAIT THAT
LASTED NEARLY THREE YEARS.

AFTER MY BITTER AND TRAUMATIC
HOSPITALIZATION, MY DOCTOR
CONFRONTED ME ABOUT
MY INCEST. I KNEW AT THAT
MOMENT THAT HE HAD
BEEN CHARMED BY MY
DAD.
"YOUR FATHER TELLS ME

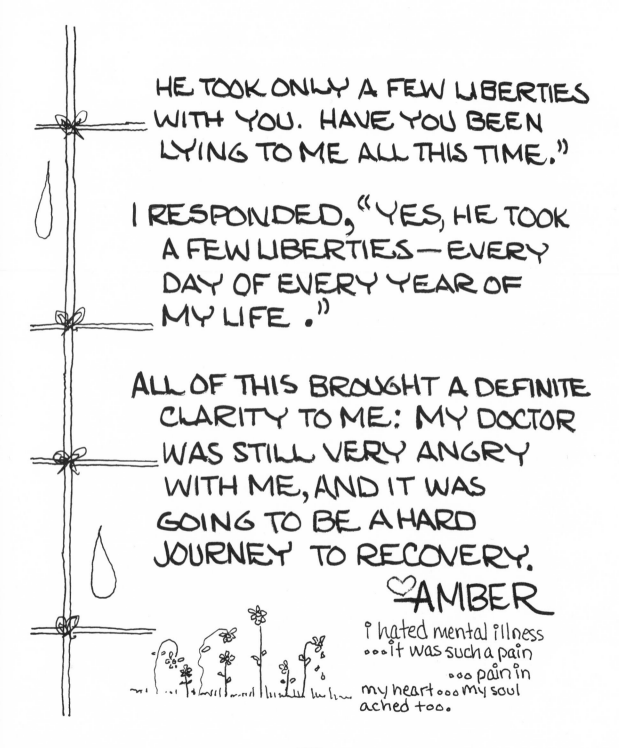

HE TOOK ONLY A FEW LIBERTIES
WITH YOU. HAVE YOU BEEN
LYING TO ME ALL THIS TIME."

I RESPONDED, "YES, HE TOOK
A FEW LIBERTIES — EVERY
DAY OF EVERY YEAR OF
MY LIFE."

ALL OF THIS BROUGHT A DEFINITE
CLARITY TO ME: MY DOCTOR
WAS STILL VERY ANGRY
WITH ME, AND IT WAS
GOING TO BE A HARD
JOURNEY TO RECOVERY.

♡AMBER

i hated mental illness
...it was such a pain
...pain in
my heart...my soul
ached too.

Val... i remember

i cannot remember her name...
and i can remember so much.

i met her at the hospital. She was
only 13 years old. i was 23.
she looked so young... plain...
vulnerable. she was there for
the injections—for the trial. she
was raped by four or five boys
... or so she said. none of us
have any credibility when we
become weak or break... not even
to each other.

i loved this girl. she was so sensitive,
so weak, so special... and she
loved me. she told me so. she gave
me a ceramic heart of blue with
my name on it... my name of Blue.
she never knew my real name,
but she loved me, and i her. i shall
never see her again. she is 33 now.
i am still 23.

Minnesota Snowflake Blessing

May a snowflake rest upon
   your weary eyelids
         and
render you the
crystal vision
of a thousand
   lifetimes.

Amber

A Minnesota Faerie
   contemplating a snowflake.

The Wondrous Dr. B.

I was overjoyed when Dr. B. diagnosed
me as manic-depressive. At
long last, I was gaining an
identity. My former doctor (I
affectionately referred to
him as the Bloated Toad of
Psychiatry) had diagnosed
me schizophrenic, yet
never discussed it with
me. I went through
nearly eight years
of therapy with him,
and all we talked about
was diets!

Manic-depression was something I could live with. To
be free of the other medications
—to be free! It was time...
time to test my creativity, my
intellect, my spirituality. To be
truly alive..

Oh, Bloated Toad, get thee back
to the swamp... I am free.

Amber

112

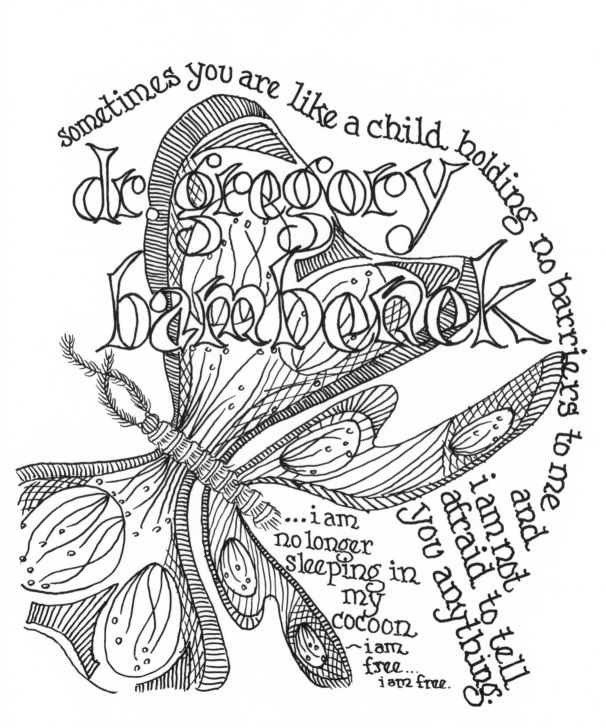

sometimes you are like a child, holding no barriers to me

dr. gregory barberek

and i am not afraid to tell you anything.

...i am no longer sleeping in my cocoon ~i am free... i am free.

113

Life in the Wilderness

During a recent session with Dr. B.,
I remarked on what might have
been had I received counseling at
the age of 7 or 8 or 9 or so. One
thing would have been certain...
the many distorted thought images
and other nonrealities would have
been somewhat curbed or, at the
very least, observed and addressed
in counseling.

As my life has unwound itself, all the
distortions have allowed themselves
to grow and become so much a
part of my being that they may
never be untangled or even
recognized.

With this realization, I can see that
I may never be truly "normal,"
whatever that is — no matter how

many therapy sessions I may have
to endure throughout my life.
In all my "growing" years, I never
saw myself as a CHILD in NEED...
in need of understanding... in
need of growth... in need of love!
I felt as long as I endured the dark
shadows of my life, there would
be indeed light near the end
of the tunnel — as in DEATH.
Instead, all I have found are mazes
in a grey haze.
I am optimistic. I will find my way
through the murky marshes
and slimy swamps of my wilderness
as long as Pooh never lets go of
my hand or I his, and we keep
on smiling.

MY REALITY

I OFTEN WONDER ABOUT THIS ENIGMA—
MENTAL ILLNESS. IT HAS INDEED
ENGULFED ME, ENRAPTURED AND
ENTICED MY SPIRIT. IT HAS AT TIMES,
TREATED ME AS A BITCH-LOVER. I HAVE
EMBRACED AND TAKEN TO MY BREAST
THE PAIN AND MISUNDERSTANDINGS
OF ALL THAT IS ABOUT ME.

I HAVE OFTEN WALLOWED IN THIS RELATIONSHIP
WITH MY MENTAL ILLNESS, REFUSING
TO REJOIN THE STRUGGLE TO MENTAL
HEALTH.

I HAVE LOVED HER DEARLY, THIS "M.I." I HAVE
GIVEN HER MY BEST. WE WERE ENEMIES,
WE WERE FRIENDS... WE PERSUADED
EACH OTHER. WE WERE FRIENDS AND
WE BELONGED TOGETHER. I HATED
HER. SHE BROUGHT THE FOG—THE FOG
OF MISJUDGMENT, OF DISTORTIONS,
OF EVENTUAL DEMISE. ... I HAVE
NOT CONQUERED ALL OF THESE.
PERHAPS I NEVER WILL. BUT I WILL

NOT SURRENDER TO THE WILL OF
THIS SMALL FRACTION OF COMPLEXITY
— THIS MENTAL ILLNESS — THIS
ATTACKER OF MY HEALTH, MY
CLARITY, MY VISIONS AND
PERCEPTIONS OF CRYSTAL
REALITY.

Vital Force

Once you have grasped
The Great Form
It will never leave
No harm can come
And whenever you roar
The Vital Force will follow

Once you have touched
The Formless Form

You will be complete
Innocent as an animal
Wise as a sage

This will seem strange
To a man
But start on the Path
The Way will prove
Inexhaustible

— Chi

Take each moment... Make it into Good and Beauty.

vow #1

Amber

I WAS ALONE...

RESPONDING TO THE EXPERIENCES I TOLD ABOUT AS AN INCEST VICTIM, MANY HAVE SIMPLY STATED, "YOU WERE NOT ALONE!" I HAVE NEVER APPRECIATED THAT RESPONSE. I HAVE CONSIDERED IT INSENSITIVE.

AS A CHILD, I ENCOUNTERED NO ONE WHO SHARED MY EXPERIENCES. IN ALL PRACTICALITY, I WAS ALONE. TODAY, AFTER KNOWING MANY OTHERS WHO HAVE EXPERIENCED INCEST AND OTHER FORMS OF CHILD ABUSE, I STILL SAY I WAS ALONE, JUST AS THEY WERE. NOTHING WILL EVER CHANGE THAT.

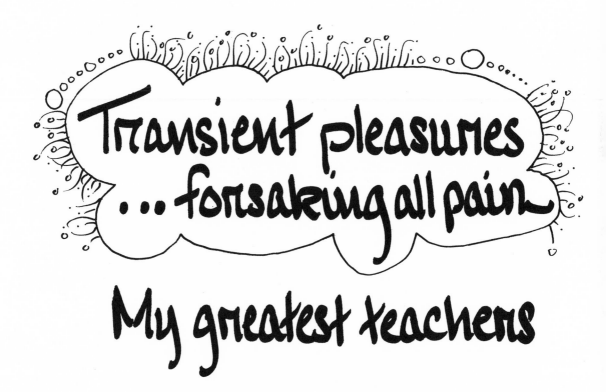

Transient pleasures
...forsaking all pain

My greatest teachers

I urge and lovingly encourage all those who have experienced the painful, humiliating and tearful murky swamp of ABUSE, to run—not walk—to the nearest Someone who will guide them back to the right path through the wilderness.

Child abuse must end... my love for humanity can overwhelm me... the little humanity I cry for and love so. May my book help bring an end to the abuse. May my book bring moments of light to those, in darkness. May our souls journey bring light to our troubled world.

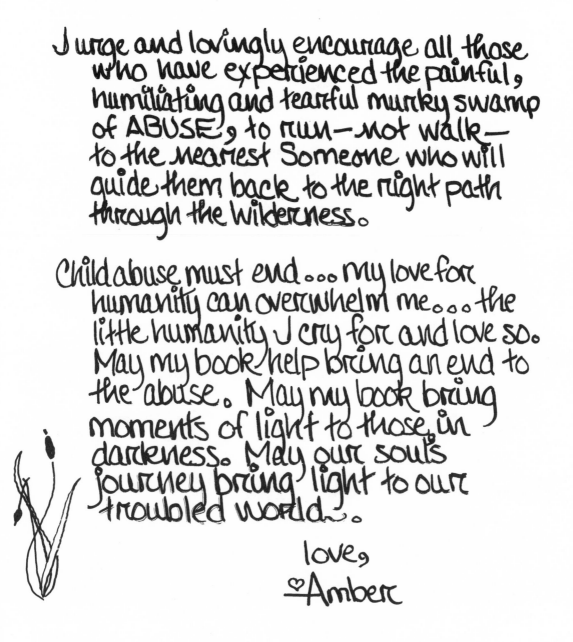

love,
♡Amber

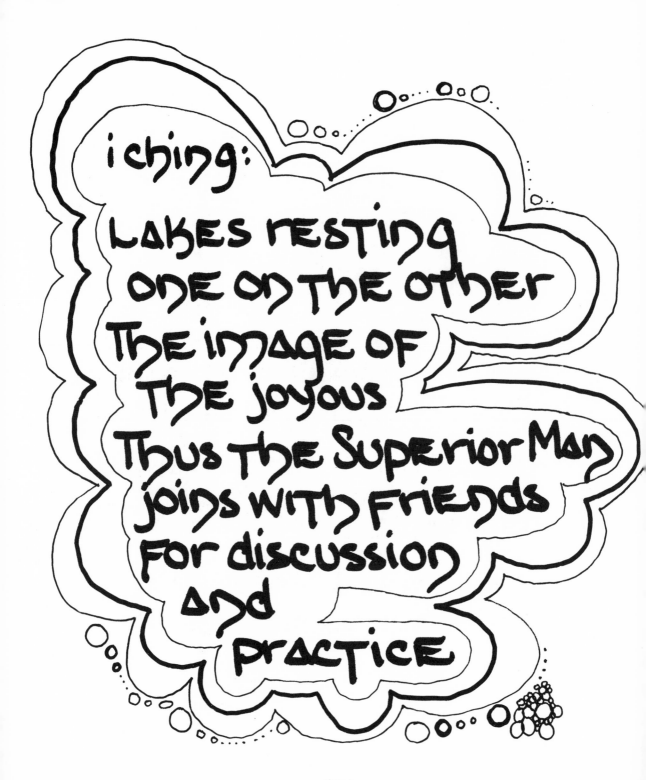

i ching:

Lakes resting
one on the other
The image of
The joyous
Thus the Superior Man
joins with friends
for discussion
and
practice

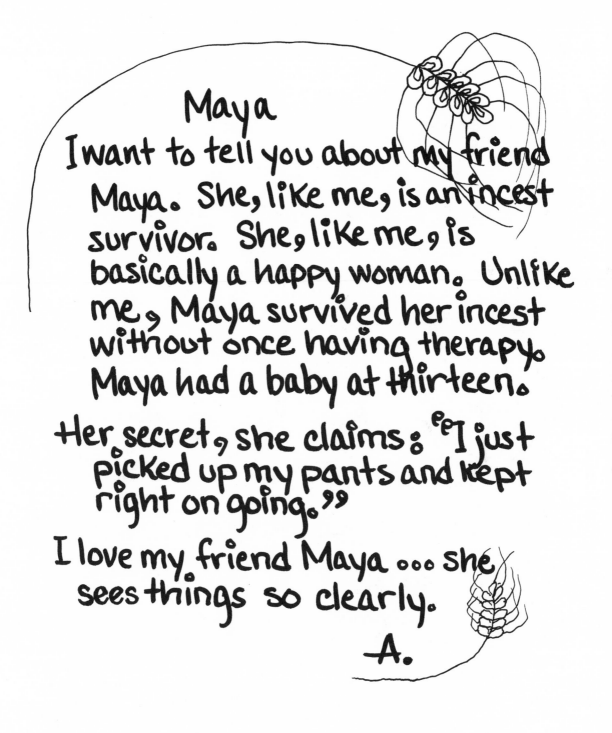

Maya

I want to tell you about my friend Maya. She, like me, is an incest survivor. She, like me, is basically a happy woman. Unlike me, Maya survived her incest without once having therapy. Maya had a baby at thirteen.

Her secret, she claims: "I just picked up my pants and kept right on going."

I love my friend Maya ... she sees things so clearly.

—A.

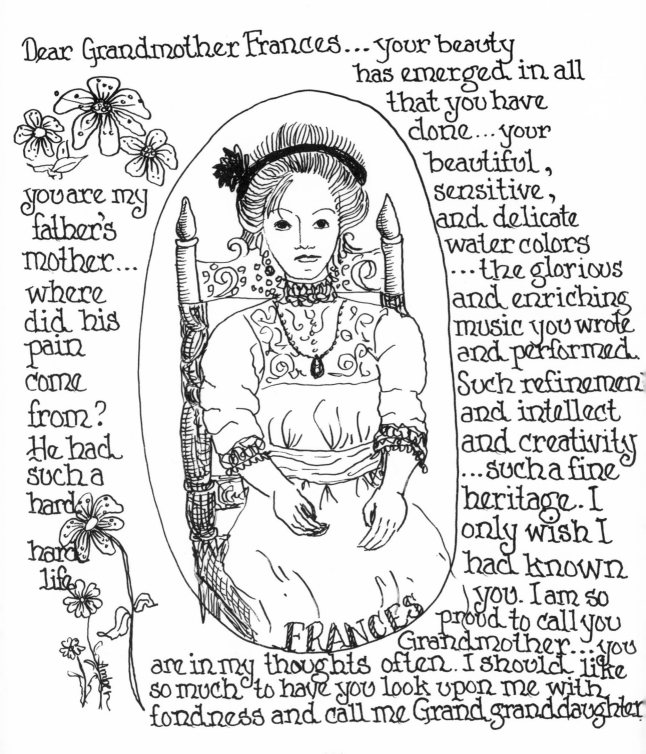

Dear Grandmother Frances... your beauty has emerged in all that you have done... your beautiful, sensitive, and delicate water colors ...the glorious and enriching music you wrote and performed. Such refinement and intellect and creativity ...such a fine heritage. I only wish I had known you. I am so proud to call you Grandmother... you

you are my father's mother... where did his pain come from? He had such a hard hard life.

FRANCES

are in my thoughts often. I should like so much to have you look upon me with fondness and call me Grand granddaughter.

128

LISTENING TO THE MUSIC OF YOUR SOUL

I cannot recall singing as a child – or as a teenager, or as a young adult. That is not to say I did not sing inside. There were many melodies and symphonies playing in my mind over and over. Lately I have allowed myself the luxury of humming and singing aloud. I have a kind and generous mind... again it tells me I am terrific. Now if only I could convince my ears.

BERYL ⚘

Beryl had always been a very special person to me. She was a resident at a nursing home where I worked as a nursing assistant. The staff and other residents openly disliked her because of her sarcasm and cynicism directed outwardly toward them. I adored her. She had such charm and personality... such beauty and class.

I had decided to give her a special valentine. As her eyesight had been failing, I decided to make a large poster of a hippopotamus and a crushed daisy.

Several months after I had given the poster to Beryl, a co-worker and I were arguing about whether it was a hippo or a pig. "Beryl," I asked, "Please tell Melanie what this is a picture of..." "Oh," she said with great emotion, "it's my home in Fergus Falls!"

Beryl, if you won't be mine i'll simply be crushed. ♥Amber

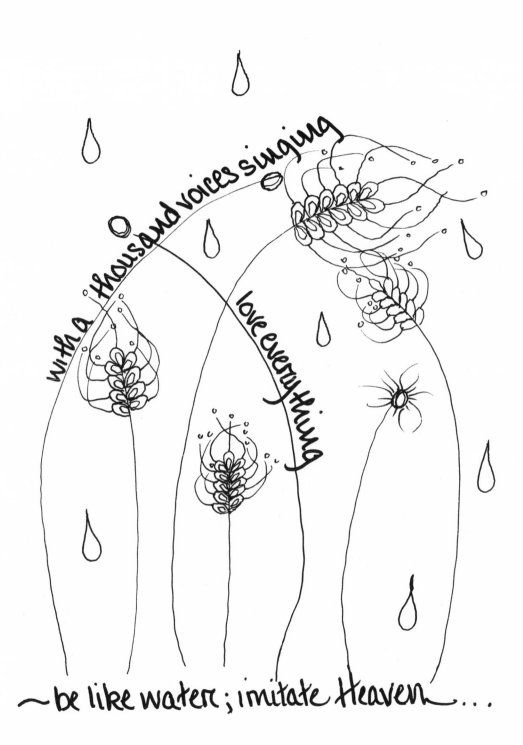

with a thousand voices singing

love everything

~ be like water; imitate Heaven ....

Sister Constantina

If I were to chose my favorite instructor in my three years at a private woman's college, I would have to say without a doubt it was little Sister Constantina. She was one of my art instructors. She received her magnificent training at the Budapest Academy of Fine Arts.

Among her many scoldings about how rude and rebellious I was as her student, her favorite was the scene in a painting class. All of our work was to be original, a rule easily understood by all... all save Mrs. Blaugh. Mrs. Blaugh insisted on copying all of her paintings. As she was a considerably older woman, this was tolerated... tolerated by everyone but me! The paint-by-number pictures were her favorite. While she painted she loved to chit-chat to anyone with an ear, or to the walls if no one would listen. Her favorite subject was God. (It was not mine.) How the good lady would go on...

THIS IS A MESSAGE FROM GOD: YOU ARE BORING!

I looked at her after one of her many ramblings and said, "Mrs. Blaugh, haven't you heard? God died of boredom years ago!" She was very upset and went off wailing to Constantina's studio.

It was not long before Sr. C. literally dragged me off to her studio by the handle of my paint brush! I knew I was about to get my "just" reward. I had without question over stepped my bounds; it was time once again to get down on my knees.

My scolding consisted of Sister telling me I was one of her few students to display definite talent and style in my work. I was throwing it all away by harassing Mrs. Blaugh, who would never benefit from the good Sister's instruction.

This lecture really didn't help... Mrs. Blaugh and I were at it again by the end of class.

Even today, several years after graduating, I see her in her studio or sometimes we shop together. Our relationship, although much friendlier, still remains teacher-student. She has dubbed herself my "spiritual guide." I still send her cards on Mother's Day.

I am certain that, when she leaves this earth, she will enter heaven, feeling she has failed with me in the "spiritual" guidance department.

I would like to point out that, although I have encountered many people with high intelligence, I have never met anyone who uses their intellect as wisely as Constantina.

—Amber 1983

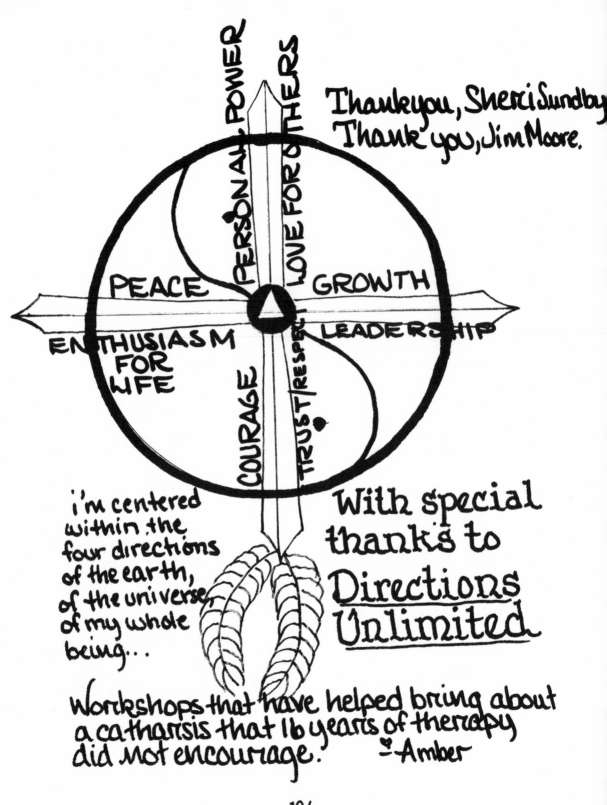

PERSONAL POWER

LOVE FOR OTHERS

Thank you, Sherci Sundby
Thank you, Jim Moore.

PEACE

GROWTH

ENTHUSIASM
FOR
LIFE

LEADERSHIP

COURAGE

TRUST/RESPECT

i'm centered
within the
four directions
of the earth,
of the universe,
of my whole
being...

With special
thanks to
Directions
Unlimited

Workshops that have helped bring about
a catharsis that 16 years of therapy
did not encourage.
♥ Amber

136

FLOYD

There is a medicine man from St. Paul whom I have admired. His name is Floyd. He is a big man and often has a fierce look about him.

I asked Floyd to look at my book. I was very much afraid to ask him, as I was certain he would reject me. He didn't. He read both portfolios. When I glanced over to see his reaction, I realized he was crying... this giant of a man was crying. When he finished he looked directly at me and said, "This is good, Amber... this is good. Don't let anyone change a thing. This is good."

ADVOCACY and STRENGTH

I am currently an advocate at a shelter for battered women and their children. I am also an advocate with a sexual assault program that works with victims of rape, child sexual assault, and other sex offenses.

These two organizations are a god-send for me personally. The fantastic women I have worked with, my "sisters," have empowered me with the fine balance of gentleness and strength necessary for my very existence.

I have always felt a need for nurturing, strength, and support from other women. I love these women dearly and feel a natural bond

with their organizations. They
have tended and nurtured me.
They have given my soul sustenance
~ I shall always remain
grateful.

♡Amber

SPECIAL♥THANKS♥TO♥SPECIAL♥PEOPLE

To All: you have supported me, challenged me, contributed to my growth, encouraged my spirituality, and have been ever-present admirers and endorsers of my creativity and reality. I acknowledge you, honor you, and love you.

♥ SHERI SUNDBY: beautiful and wise, my agent, confidante and friend;

DENNIS KALKBRENNER: my closest
♥ friend and mentor, a writer of intense beauty and pain;

MELANIE TROSBY: she has been with me in good spirit since I began my book nine years ago. She is so dear to
♥ me... I love her;

♥ BERNIE AND SANDY: another part of
♥ my support group; they make me laugh;

JIM DIMMERS: a beautiful man, a beautiful artist, and truly someone beautiful to know;

140

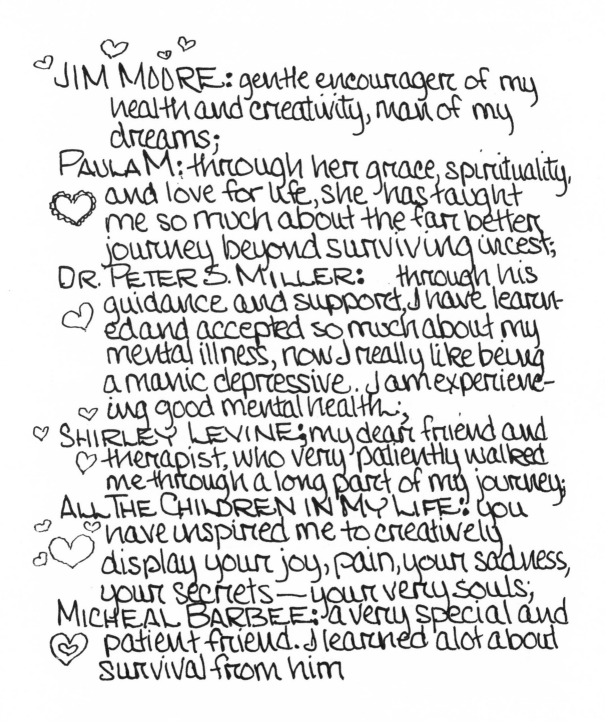

JIM MOORE: gentle encourager of my
health and creativity, man of my
dreams;

PAULA M: through her grace, spirituality,
and love for life, she has taught
me so much about the far better
journey beyond surviving incest;

DR. PETER S. MILLER: through his
guidance and support, I have learned and accepted so much about my
mental illness, now I really like being
a manic depressive. I am experiencing good mental health;

SHIRLEY LEVINE; my dear friend and
therapist, who very patiently walked
me through a long part of my journey;

ALL THE CHILDREN IN MY LIFE: you
have inspired me to creatively
display your joy, pain, your sadness,
your secrets — your very souls;

MICHEAL BARBEE: a very special and
patient friend. I learned alot about
survival from him

For All Those Special People Who Have Freed My Soul ♡

To: the most beautiful dolphin in the sea

From: a somewhat mystic female

As the fish while eye to eye to the butterfly said:
yes, I have freed your soul but tell me... in all your
flights of absolute freedom, how is this so?

Said the butterfly to the fish:
because, dear one, you allowed it
to be... me to be... just me
and, for this most beautiful of gifts,
I say to you:
set me free
set me free
and I will always return to thee.
let me go... watch me grow
...and with warmth, and kindness,
and pride and so...
The gentlest of gentle understanding
that you have shown me
will return
to
thee.
love, Amber

142

Minnesota Faerie becoming
the butterfly

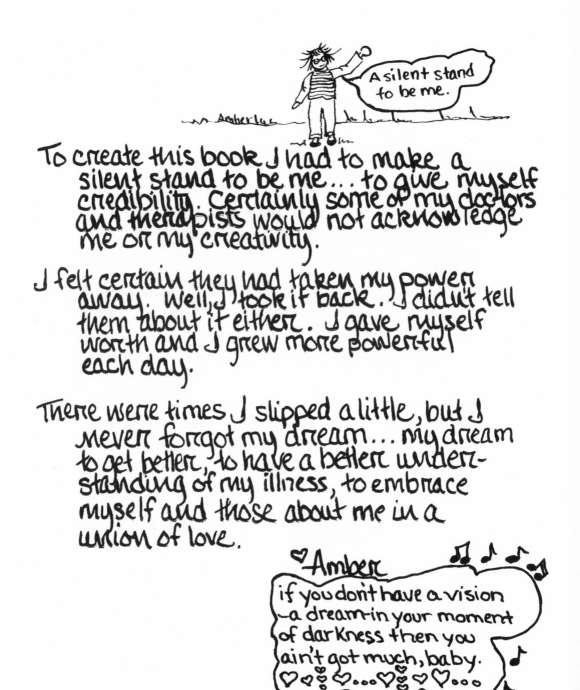

A silent stand to be me.

To create this book I had to make a silent stand to be me... to give myself credibility. Certainly some of my doctors and therapists would not acknowledge me or my creativity.

I felt certain they had taken my power away. Well, I took it back. I didn't tell them about it either. I gave myself worth and I grew more powerful each day.

There were times I slipped a little, but I never forgot my dream... my dream to get better, to have a better understanding of my illness, to embrace myself and those about me in a union of love.

♡ Amber

if you don't have a vision —a dream—in your moment of darkness then you ain't got much, baby.
♡ ♡ °°° ♡ ♡ ♡ °°°

All my life i have
wanted something
my very own....

something to cherish,
something to nourish...
to educate... to love.

And i have found
this "something"
deep, deep inside
myself... that
"something" is me.

♡Amber

Amber

"AMONG THE DAISIES AND THE FORGET-ME-NOTS"

it has seemed
to take forever
for me to be
free

. . . .free to be just me.

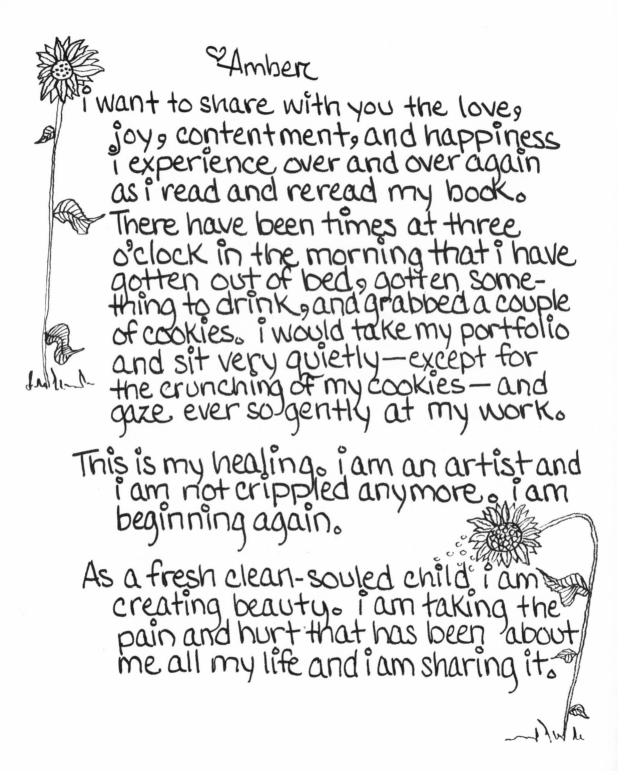

♡Amber♡

i want to share with you the love,
joy, contentment, and happiness
i experience over and over again
as i read and reread my book.
There have been times at three
o'clock in the morning that i have
gotten out of bed, gotten something to drink, and grabbed a couple
of cookies. i would take my portfolio
and sit very quietly—except for
the crunching of my cookies—and
gaze ever so gently at my work.

This is my healing. i am an artist and
i am not crippled anymore. i am
beginning again.

As a fresh clean-souled child i am
creating beauty. i am taking the
pain and hurt that has been about
me all my life and i am sharing it.

i am giving you an experience of this pain as i best remember it... i am giving it all away. It won't return to me because i am filling all those spaces with the same love, joy, contentment, and happiness that i received just creating my book and sharing it with others.

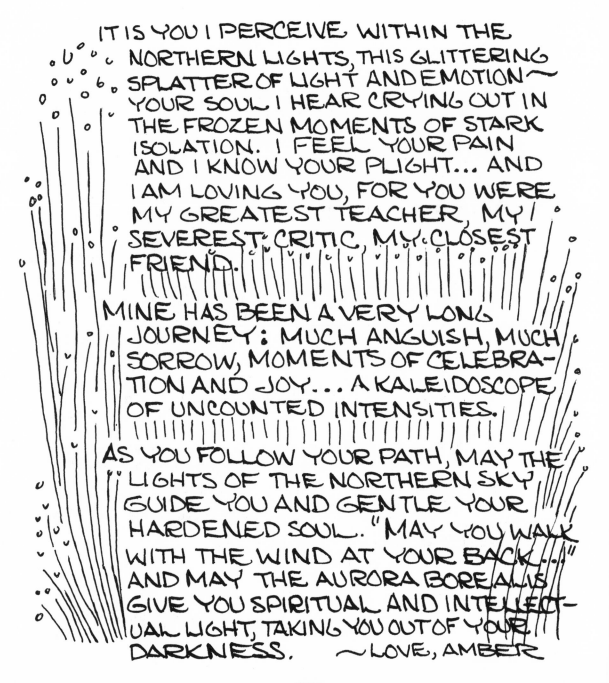

ACKNOWLEDGING MY PERPETRATOR

IT IS YOU I PERCEIVE WITHIN THE NORTHERN LIGHTS, THIS GLITTERING SPLATTER OF LIGHT AND EMOTION~ YOUR SOUL I HEAR CRYING OUT IN THE FROZEN MOMENTS OF STARK ISOLATION. I FEEL YOUR PAIN AND I KNOW YOUR PLIGHT... AND I AM LOVING YOU, FOR YOU WERE MY GREATEST TEACHER, MY SEVEREST CRITIC, MY CLOSEST FRIEND.

MINE HAS BEEN A VERY LONG JOURNEY: MUCH ANGUISH, MUCH SORROW, MOMENTS OF CELEBRA-TION AND JOY... A KALEIDOSCOPE OF UNCOUNTED INTENSITIES.

AS YOU FOLLOW YOUR PATH, MAY THE "LIGHTS OF THE NORTHERN SKY GUIDE YOU AND GENTLE YOUR HARDENED SOUL. "MAY YOU WALK WITH THE WIND AT YOUR BACK..." AND MAY THE AURORA BOREALIS GIVE YOU SPIRITUAL AND INTELLECT-UAL LIGHT, TAKING YOU OUT OF YOUR DARKNESS.   ~LOVE, AMBER

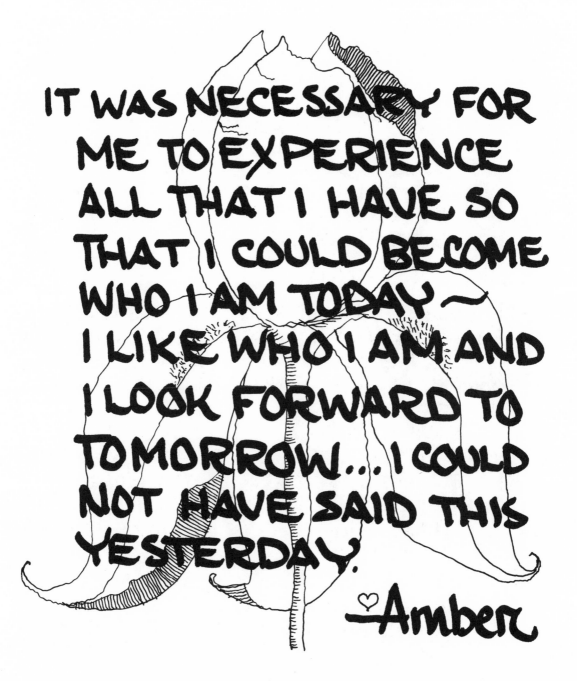

IT WAS NECESSARY FOR
ME TO EXPERIENCE
ALL THAT I HAVE, SO
THAT I COULD BECOME
WHO I AM TODAY ~
I LIKE WHO I AM AND
I LOOK FORWARD TO
TOMORROW... I COULD
NOT HAVE SAID THIS
YESTERDAY.

♡ Amber

Daddy, please say you're sorry. Love, Amber